MW01235344

Fishing
in the Sky:

The Education of Namory Keita

Fishing in the Sky:

The Education of Namory Keita

Donald Lawder

No part of this publication may be reproduced or transmitted in any form
or by any means, electronic, or mechanical, including photocopy,
recording, scanning or any information storage retrieval system, without
explicit permission in writing from the Author.

© Copyright 1997 by Donald Lawder
First e-reads publication 1999
www.e-reads.com
ISBN 0-7592-3888-X

For Donny, Bruce, Amy, Linda, Wally, and Donna

Acknowledgments

I can't have been as wholly undeserving as I sometimes think, for during my life I have made and kept a number of wonderful friends, some of whom have helped make this book possible. It was Stephen Dunn who first insisted that I give literary form to my personal observations and experiences in Mali and who patiently commented on my early drafts. Richard Gardner hides an abiding love of poetry and art behind the gruff exterior of a data-processing wizard; when I left permanently for Mali, he surprised me with the gift of the computer on which this book was written. The novelist Edward Hower stayed with me for three days in Bamako while visiting a near relative among my fellow volunteers; he took back with him a copy of this manuscript to show to his publisher, with the result you see here.

Like the volunteers in their charge, the local officials of Peace Corps— Country Directors and Assistant Directors—come and go every few years. The day-to-day work of running the operation is done by Malian nationals, and these have been uniformly helpful to me. Kader Traoré, who is responsible for handling the mail, has gone out of his way to make sure I received letters and packages addressed to me, even after my official connection with Peace Corps was ended. Mamadou Coulibaly ("Mama") relieved me of any worries I might have had about the permanence of my residence in Mali by securing for me a five-year visa with a promise of renewal. Marie Claire Jubin, the Director's secretary, has helped me in innumerable ways, as have a host of others, including Sire Diallo, Sidi Yattara, Sambou Konaté, and Kadidia Dienta. The spelling of Malian names and Bambara words was a problem at the beginning, and I am grateful for the help of Mamadou Samaké and Veronica Coulibaly, who screened my early drafts for errors in this and in the interpretation of certain Bambara customs. To my many friends, colleagues, and former students in Mali, my debt should be self-evident in the following pages. Finally, I want to add a special note of gratitude to my son Wally who has stood loyally by me during all my travails and has made a number of useful suggestions for the final draft.

Table of Contents

BOOK I. (1983–1986)

Foreword		xi
Chapter 1	La Maison Des Jeunes	3
Chapter 2	Moribabougou	10
Chapter 3	Born Again	20
Chapter 4	Making a Home in the City	26
Chapter 5	L'Ecôle Normale Supèrieure	43
Chapter 6	Aisha	54
Chapter 7	God in the Classroom and Other Anecdotes	68
Chapter 8	Dreams and Near Disasters	81
Chapter 9	Partings	88

BOOK II (1988–94)

Chapter 10	Return of the Prodigal	99
Chapter 11	Will I Ever Get to Timbuktoo?	108
Chapter 12	Playing Grandfather	117
Chapter 13	Explosion!	129
Chapter 14	"The Best of Times . . . The Worst of Times"	136
Chapter 15	Grandfather For Real	144
Chapter 16	"Bless You Aminata"	155
Afterword		159

Foreword

This is a thin book to contain so many years of life and discovery. A lifetime, it seems now. A second lifetime.

Originally, this was not to be a book at all but a series of letters to family and friends describing my day-to-day adventures and encounters in a world that hitherto had existed only in my imagination. I was proud—too proud, I see now—of my ability at age sixty-six to thrive under conditions that were daunting young men and women a third my age. Thanks to my sympathetic audience, I actually conceived of myself as a kind of hero, and I believed that whatever interested them was bound to interest everyone else.

I myself knew I was not a hero at all. In fact, my adventure in Africa was undertaken for the most cowardly of reasons, as an alternative to a decade or more of checker games in a senior center. Weary at the futility of my work as an advertising copywriter, and disheartened by my failures as a husband and a father, I had taken advantage of a flexible work schedule to go back to school and prepare myself for a "golden-age career" as a college English teacher. But I soon found that the demand for sixty-five-year-old English teachers was inconsiderable.

Then I learned that the Peace Corps was looking for teachers to work as volunteers in some of the poorer countries of the world. It paid these volunteers only enough to subsist on, but what was important to me was that the work seemed useful and there was no upper age limit. I fired off an application and two months later, after an interview and a physical, I received an official invitation to teach English to French-speaking young Africans at the national teachers' college of the Republic of Mali in West Africa.

The intervening years, most of which were spent as a teacher of English at L'Ecôle Normale Supérieure in the impoverished Republic of Mali, have taught me that the real hero of the story was never myself, but the extraordinary people among whom I lived. I got to know them well—as students and colleagues, as friends and as lovers. I was adopted into a Malian family and given a Malian name. I fell in and out of love with an African woman less than half my age, prayed at the mosques, held hands with dying friends, and threw my own handfuls of earth into their open graves. I was eyewitness to the first democratic revolution in Africa. I serve now as "grandfather" and head of household for an African family of six children from four to twenty-four years of age.

In the beginning, I expected to stay in this kind but ill-favored country for no more than the required two years, but out of love and wonderment I have stayed for over a dozen. Ultimately, what began as a series of personal letters has become instead the memoir of a love affair with Africa and a kind of hymn to the glorious diversity of humankind.

All the happenings described here actually happened, and all of the people are real. However, to protect individuals from embarrassment, I have here and there changed names and details.

Book I
(1983-86)

A Celebration
of Differences

Glory be to God for dappled things—
  For skies of couple-colour as a brinded cow;
    For rose-moles all in stipple upon trout that swim;
Fresh-firecoal chestnut-falls; finches' wings;
  Landscape plotted and pieced—fold, fallow, and plough;
    And all trades, their gear and tackle and trim.
All things counter, original, spare, strange;
  Whatever is fickle, freckled (who knows how?)
    With swift, slow; sweet, sour; adazzle, dim;
  He fathers forth whose beauty is beyond change:
    Praise Him.

Gerard Manley Hopkins

1

La Maison des Jeunes

Early in the afternoon of July 8, one week after my sixty-sixth birthday and a few hours out of Paris, Lynn Griffith called to me from her window seat across the aisle, "Hey, Don, we must be over Mali! I see the Sahara down there!"

A serious young woman from Wyoming, tall and fairly large-boned with perhaps a few drops of Native American blood, Lynn was one of my early favorites in our contingent of Peace Corps volunteers, perhaps because, at twenty-six, she was one of the oldest. After college, Lynn had tried a few inconsequential jobs and, when she found them leading her nowhere she especially wanted to go, joined the Peace Corps; she had a wonderful sense of starting over.

I leaned over and craned for my first look at the country where I, too, was to spend the next twenty-four months, but there was nothing to see. Nothing, that is, but a great ocean of beige stretching from horizon to horizon, texture-less and vacant. Half of Mali, from its northwestern borders with Mauritania and Algeria eastward to the ancient cities of Timbuktoo and Gao, is like this, peopled only by passing caravans and a few thousand nomadic families. Together, we stared fascinated for hours and saw never a hint of shadow.

3

I tried to visualize the kinds of lives that might go on in that featureless desert, but all I could bring to mind were childhood pictures of conquest and adventure—*Lawrence of Arabia*, Chinese Gordon, Ronald Colman with the French Foreign Legion in the film *Beau Geste*—all the great jingoistic books and movies. I thought of my destination in the Dark Continent—the "heart of darkness" below the desert. What did I know of Africa and Africans besides a few exciting stories of jungles and lions—hapless Frances MacComber with a bullet in his skull—outnumbered British mercenaries falling before the black dervishes at Khartoum—wild Stanley gunning his way down the Congo in search of fame and Livingston?

I knew, of course, that I wouldn't find lions in Mali, nor mobs of whirling dervishes either. I was going to be living and working in a country where the natural graces of rain and fertile soil are so scarce that even the feeble help I and my fellow American volunteers could offer would make us absurdly welcome. Still, my bookish childhood kept haunting me, shaming me with its distorted perceptions.

The seat-belt light came on and I felt the plane descend toward Mali's capital city of Bamako. I glimpsed a blur of gray-green, then a sleek, professional-looking control tower and, as we taxied, a conventionally shiny airport building with a glass-walled restaurant on its second floor. Like Topeka, Kansas, I thought. Like anywhere.

Once we alighted, I knew I was wrong. Nothing about this place was shiny. Everything—everything—was the reddish color of clay—the grass, the occasional trees, even the restaurant windows. The parking lot was almost deserted. On a field large enough to handle the biggest jets, ours was the only visible plane.

A score of large black men in flowing robes of many colors—apparently government officials or visiting dignitaries—preceded us importantly off the plane, and then we fifty-odd volunteers, each eager to place both feet on African soil, swarmed onto the tarmac. John Zarafanides, the local Peace Corps director, and some members of his staff were on hand to greet us. So was the U.S. ambassador, a soft-spoken, sprawly sort of man with unpressed trousers, unshined shoes, and a face that reminded me of Howdy Doody. He spoke for about two minutes in a light Minnesota accent, and I felt he was the right man for such a place. The temperature must have been a hundred and one.

If anything, it was hotter and dirtier inside the terminal. The glass-walled restaurant that had looked so tempting from a distance was empty and apparently closed. There was no newsstand, no gift shop, not even a Coke machine, just a score of officials in olive drab uniforms listlessly directing traffic, and a couple of old men with carvings to sell.

4

Evidently the Peace Corps had made some sort of arrangement with the military government, for we volunteers were waved through customs uninspected and were out of the building in less than half an hour. Once in the street we stowed ourselves and our luggage in three or four bashées (middle-sized pickup trucks with side benches and canvas tops like the weapons carriers I rode in the army forty years before) and headed for the center of Bamako.

Now for the first time, Bamako began to hint at the exotic side I'd heard and read about—small villages of thatch-roofed mud houses, humpbacked cattle, miniature donkeys as comical as Giapetto's pulling loads that towered twice their height above them, women in brilliantly colored ankle-length robes, bearing on their heads platters of bananas and baskets of vegetables, green oranges, and what appeared to be laundry.

As we approached the city we found ourselves part of a procession of vehicles—battered Peugeots and Citroens, shiny black Mercedes, twenty-five-year-old Volkswagens, and scores of vans, trucks, and overloaded taxis competing doggedly for space with what must have been hundreds of bicycles, motor-cycles, and motor scooters.

At last, after ten or a dozen miles of this traffic, we came to the famous Niger river, pronounced by everyone here in the French fashion, "ni-ZHAIRE." The Niger is one of the great rivers of the world, traversing almost the entire width of West Africa and nourishing the dry land in the same way the Nile nourishes Egypt. For most of its course, the Niger flows so slowly that one of the great puzzles to nineteenth-century explorers was, Which way does the river flow, westward toward the Atlantic or southeastward to the Gulf of Guinea? For some reason, they failed to learn this from the fishermen along the river, and the direction of the Niger's flow remained an enigma until a Belgian named Speakes worked his way to the vicinity of Bamako, where the current is a bit swifter, and saw that the flow was to the southeast. In the process, he caught malaria and died; he is buried not far from Bamako, in Koulikoro.

However impressive the Niger may appear in atlases, it looked pretty ordinary here, and the low bridge across it was no more spectacular, though perhaps longer, than the Post Road bridge across the Saugatuck River in Westport, Connecticut. As soon as we crossed, our driver turned and pulled up at a big, three-story masonry building surrounded by enormous kapok trees standing tall on their roots like a squadron of Tolkien's Ents preparing to charge.

La Maison des Jeunes, or Youth House, the place was called, and it was here the Peace Corps had arranged for us to spend our first week in Africa. Built by

5

the French during the colonial regime, La Maison was once probably modern and solid, but was now falling apart because of lack of maintenance. Windows were broken, doors didn't latch, toilets had no seats, shower drains were clogged, and the whole effect was of appalling decadence and decay. Worst of all, the Peace Corps had packed us in like herrings in a barrel: My room contained ten cots placed six to eight inches apart so I had to creep sidewise into bed. The shower room was coed. Defecation was performed standing up or squatting. No place for the squeamish.

Once our duffels were unloaded and partly unpacked, we gathered in the yard to listen to Rebecca, our pretty Peace Corps Medical Officer, give us a quick review of elementary health precautions: Don't drink untreated water (bacteria and parasites); don't eat ice cream sold on the street (tuberculosis); take Chloroquin tablets religiously (malaria); and use condoms (available free and in a choice of colors) during intercourse. It was about five o'clock, and above her voice I could hear the hoarse cries of what sounded like a flock of starlings in a roost. I looked up, and there, wheeling among the branches above us and thick as insects around a lamp, were hundreds of giant bats; their wings seemed a foot and a half across. These were fruit bats, I learned, and they don't zig and zag like the bats I knew back home, for they don't eat insects at all, just dates, mangoes, and other fruits. I made a tape of their sounds.

Out of consideration for bodies six hours out of step with African clocks, we were allowed to sleep late our first morning in Bamako, and when I awoke it must have been nearly nine o'clock. I wrapped myself in a towel and waddled along the balcony to the coed shower, then dressed and went outside to listen to the chatter of the bats. They fly about constantly except during the hottest part of the day, between noon and three o'clock, when they fold themselves into their wings and hang head downward from the branches.

But it was soon clear that we weren't brought to Africa to muse on bats or other bits of local color. Breakfast was a fast hustle of French bread and Malian-style coffee—a quarter teaspoon of Nescafe and three soupspoons of sweetened condensed milk in a tin cup of hot water, like a hot malted milk with too much syrup in it—and by nine forty-five we were out under the date palms for our first training session. Life, we were told, will get tougher: classes from eight to noon; a three-hour break for lunch and siesta; classes again until six in the evening; training sessions most evenings as well.

This first morning was Orientation, and it began with the introduction of our "professors," the young men and women who were to spend the summer preparing us for whatever it was we were expected to do. All of them were Malians, except for Monica Kerrigan, the snub-nosed Irish-American consul-

6

tant who'd been brought over from the U.S. to coordinate our training, and a stupendous young redhead named Becky who had just finished her own stint as a Peace Corps volunteer and was helping out with the logistics; when not rushing about getting things done, Becky kept busy cleaning pus from an ulcerated sore on her left calf.

The Malians were a surprise to me. I don't know what I had imagined they would be like, if I imagined anything, but they certainly didn't remind me of black Americans. First of all, they were, with just a couple of exceptions, really black—black the way a freshly polished iron stove is black. Yet the faces of most of them were not what white Americans like myself have been taught to call "negroid." They seemed to be, and in fact they were, of many ethnic types, and despite their color the features of some of them could scarcely be told from those of a European.

Their manner, likewise, didn't fit my romantic stereotypes, and I could see that whatever might have remained of the old tribal ways had been well veneered by four generations of French colonial occupation and a further twenty years as an "independent" satellite of the great powers; nothing of the primitive was apparent in their behavior. During the school year, most of these instructors were full-time lycée teachers or graduate students of education at ENSup (the school where I was scheduled to start teaching in just three months), and because of this, and perhaps especially because Mali was their country, their own turf, they were completely at ease in their professorial roles.

The instructor in charge of this first morning's session was a light-skinned, loose-jointed Malian whom everyone called "Sam" because his last name was Samakè (SAM-a-kay). Of all our trainers, Sam was the only one I might have mistaken for an American; his cowboy slouch and easy, expansive gestures had nothing of the Hollywood African about them. Sam was in charge of what is called "cross-cultural" training, and apparently his first responsibility was to see that we learned enough of the history, traditions, and customs of Mali to keep from insulting people by accident.

There would be no forks and spoons in the bush, so we were taught to eat our rice as the Malians do, with our fingers from a common bowl. There is an etiquette for this. The family gathers on low stools around the food, the men and boys in one ring, the women and younger children in another. The chief of the family washes his hands in a bowl of water and then passes the water around the circle so that everyone in turn can wash; he also gives the sign to begin. The meal is eaten ravenously and in silence. Each person must eat only from that part of the bowl that is in front of him, and only with the right hand. This last is especially important, as the left hand is reserved for cleaning oneself with water after defecating; toilet paper is not considered effective and, in any case, is almost never available. There are other taboos against the use of the left hand, such as shaking hands and offering gifts or money.

At lunch we had a chance to practice all this, dipping our right hands diffidently into a great bowl of white rice into which had been stirred some kind of tomato-based sauce with a few chunks of meat. I learned that the best way to keep from using my left hand accidentally was to sit on it. After lunch, I watched half a dozen small and very ragged boys creep into the yard with slingshots; one of them brought down a sleeping bat and skinned it.

In the afternoon, we had our first language lesson. During their first three months of training, all volunteers in Mali are expected to become fluent in at least two languages—French, the official language of the country, and Bambara, the *lingua franca* spoken by about 60 percent of the population. These first few days were being devoted to Bambara, and this afternoon we learned the traditional ceremony of greeting.

Back home, we say "good morning" or "good afternoon," or maybe just "hi," and the other person simply returns the greeting or says something like "fine, how are you?" Here, such shortcut greetings would be considered disrespectful, even if merely buying something from a merchant on the street. There is an established ritual, with variations, in which each inquires in turn after the health of every member of the other's family, and it can go on seemingly forever. Gaussou Mariko, our Bambara teacher, told us that the more people one asks about the more respect one shows, and respect is what the people of this unlucky country have learned to cherish and to share.

The ritual responses are especially interesting. For one thing, they are sexually loaded. The male response to a greeting, *mba!*, is a kind of combination between a grunt and a belch; it begins with a short, deep *m* and ends with an explosive *ba!*—a real billygoat sound. The female response, *nsè*, is much less assertive, almost a whinny. And apparently no one ever admits to being "fine": one is "at peace" or has "no problems."

Just as we were winding up classes for the day, I was startled to hear tom-toms beating at the far corner of the open court. There was a small stage there for productions of various sorts, and a group of young men and women in their bright everyday robes were loosening up for a dance. It turned out they were members of the Bamako District Dance Troupe, amateurs who were rehearsing a program of traditional dances for the upcoming Muslim feast of Ramadan. The dancers weren't in ritual costume, and there was a lot of laughter and horsing around—not at all a finished performance—but the movements were rhythmical, stylized, and vigorous. I had no way of knowing whether this was the real face of Africa I was seeing, but it was certainly a real face.

Dinner was rice with a spicy tomato sauce, eaten, of course, with the fingers. Afterwards, we had just seated ourselves in the courtyard to begin another class in Bambara when violent gusts began to shake the trees overhead and to bring leaves, fruits, and small branches tumbling down on us. "Rain!" cried Becky, and we hurriedly picked up our chairs and followed her in a wild dash to the relative safety of a tin-roofed shed, or hangar nearby.

And rain it was! No cozy pitter-patter on the roof, in fact no identifiable sound of rain at all, just a continuous crashing sound, as if all the gods of Africa had decided to empty a skyful of water on our heads. The uproar continued for at least half an hour while we tried as best we could to hear what Gaussou was teaching us. My fellows at the edge of the shelter, who were being soaked simultaneously by wind-borne rain and splashing mud, began making loud, uncomfortable noises of their own and, eventually, Sam told Gaussou to give up. We waited and listened.

The Malian year is not conveniently separated into the short and roughly equal seasons of spring, summer, fall, and winter. Instead, there are just two grossly unequal seasons, a short rainy one, and a long dry one. The rainy season usually begins in mid-June and continues to about the end of September. It is the one fecund season of the year, the season for planting and cultivating; during the following eight months, most of the country receives scarcely a drop of rain, and that period is called, logically, the "dry season." We had arrived just after the beginning of the rains.

The rain ceased as suddenly as it had begun, and the sun glowed hazily through the super-saturated air. Within minutes, as if by miracle, the earth dried, leaving only a few muddy puddles scattered here and there. I was told we could expect downpours like this three or four times each week, perhaps oftener, for the next three months.

At seven o'clock, the Bamako Dance Troupe arrived to begin another rehearsal and this time invited those of us watching to join them. A number of my fellows jumped at the chance and were soon hopping gaily about the stage. I, too, thought of accepting but chickened out at the last moment. It had been more than forty years since I last dared trust my uncoordinated feet on a dance floor. Maybe next year, I told myself as I listened to the commanding drums.

9

2

Moribabougou

L ate on a Friday afternoon, after a truncated week in the pesthole of La
Maison des Jeunes and a bone-jarring hour out of Bamako, our little
caravan of pickups and four-by-fours pulled off the rough tar road to
Koulikoro and rolled to a stop before a small, tin-roofed cement hut.
Alongside the hut, which was evidently a kind of general store, were arranged
baskets and trays of fruits, vegetables, and whole fish, each guarded by an
elderly black woman dressed in one of the highly colored cotton robes that
are the common garb of both men and women in this part of Africa. A gray
gecko lizard poked its flattened head out of a crevice in the hut and, after a
laconic look round, pulled it back into the dark interior.

"Welcome to Moribabougou!" called out Sam, our loose-limbed coordina-
tor of cross-cultural training.

Curiosity spiced with trepidation, all thirty-five of us new and
unblooded Peace Corps volunteers clambered out, eager for a sight of the
village that would be our home for the next three months. I felt a tug on the
canvas sack containing the few possessions I had brought with me from
America and looked down to see a ragged, gap-toothed boy of about seven
or eight struggling to take it from me. Conditioned by my suburban

upbringing and decades of devotion to Eric Ambler and Graham Greene, I struggled back.

Sam laughed at my concern. "Let him take it. He's just trying to help you." I looked down at two oversize brown eyes peering uncertainly back from under a pair of thick, curly black lashes.

"*Allons!*" I conceded and, grinning proudly at this acknowledgment of his special status, my little helper beckoned to one of the larger boys to join him. Together, they shouldered the bag and led me and my compatriots back across the road and into the yard of a small school. There, it seemed, nearly half the village's population of three thousand had gathered. Tom-toms were beating and, as we new American volunteers came into sight, several hundred of the older children formed themselves into a gantlet—two cheering rows through which we were obliged to dance our way to the reed shelter that had been put up to shade us from the sun. Idrissa, as my friend was named, set my bag in a reserved area alongside and mounted guard.

Once we volunteers were settled on grass mats, the chief of the village, an elderly doctor wearing horn-rimmed glasses and a bright blue, ankle-length robe called a *grand boubou*, welcomed us with a brief speech in French. He then introduced in turn the schoolmaster, the leader of the women's society, and the village's two oldest, hence most honored, men. These last spoke to us in Bambara, which although all of us were learning, none of us yet understood.

Again the tom-toms began beating, and suddenly a magnificently polka-dotted representation of a cow galloped into the open space before us and cavorted wildly about. The beat of the tom-toms quickened and soon another creature, larger and more savage-looking, charged in. Was this a lion come to kill the poor cow? No, for after a lot of suspicious stomping and pawing about, the two beasts became friends, and the dance ended with them standing on their hind legs embracing one another. It was, Sam explained, a traditional ceremony of welcome, symbolized by the mating of cow and bull.

After the dance came the real business of the day, the assignment of volunteers to the families that had agreed to "adopt" them for the next twelve weeks. One by one, the family chiefs—all men—were called to the front and introduced to their new offspring. My name fell about halfway down the list and my "father" turned out to be a feeble and unsmiling old man (actually about five years younger than myself) named Birama Keita (KAY-ta). We shook hands, and Birama seemed uncomfortable with his position in the limelight. Idrissa and his helper took up my bag, and I followed wordlessly through the rutted streets to the mud-walled compound that was to be my first home in Africa.

The Keita clan is a large one, and members of a half-dozen or more families of Keita were gathered in the tiny court to greet me, among them at least

11

thirty children. I did my best to follow the guidelines Peace Corps had laid down for us during our first few days in Mali to ensure that none of us insulted our hosts by the accidental violation of their customs, but the scene was too confusing, and I was obliged to fall back on just looking warm and respectful in the best ways I could.

This stratagem, When you don't know what to do, just add an extra dollop of respect, served me well all my years in Mali and wouldn't be a bad one for everyone to follow everywhere. The fewer material goods people possess, the more substantial their immaterial possessions—their dignity and self-respect—seem to them. If you honor them too much, you will be quickly forgiven; if too little, the insult may be permanent.

At the moment I was writing this, barely a dozen years after my first encounter with the Keita family, American cities were again running with fire and blood because we Americans had not yet learned this elementary lesson: Respect is as necessary to mankind as food and water.

Between 70 and 80 percent of Malians are Muslim and, since the Qur'an permits each man as many as four wives, the typical Malian family is enormous. Six surviving children per wife is not uncommon (a lucky mother might have ten or more), and the typical household will also include any number of cousins, second cousins, uncles, in-laws, grandparents, and grandchildren. I was much surprised, therefore, to find that my own immediate family would consist only of old Birama, his wife Mariam—a good-looking, full-breasted woman of, I guessed, about forty or forty-five—and one unspeaking three-year-old boy, Modibo, Modibo, I learned later, was not their own but had been "lent" to them by a relative after the custom here, for apparently Mariam and Birama were unable to have children of their own.

Gradually the crowd thinned, leaving mostly the children behind, and Mariam guided me around the walled compound (it couldn't really be called a house) in which my room was located. The enclosed court was of bare earth about fifty feet square, with a small mango tree just off center. At one end was what might be called the house proper—a narrow building built of cement block after the French colonial style, not of mud as I had been led to expect, and with a long verandah from which four doors led off to individual sleeping rooms. On the opposite end was, in one corner, a small mud-walled, thatch-roofed cooking house, and in the other, a mud-walled latrine. Barely thirty feet from the latrine was the well from which the family drew its water for washing, cooking, and drinking, and I was immediately thankful for the supply of boiled and filtered water the Peace Corps had provided for volunteers to drink.

My own room was one of the four and had its own corrugated metal door opening off the verandah. To protect volunteers from mosquitoes, Peace

Corps had installed screens in our sleeping rooms, and these were to be left behind as fringe benefits; they were the only compensation our host families would receive for housing us. Peace Corps had also furnished each volunteer with an iron cot, a cotton mattress, a mosquito net, and a trunk of painted tin in which to stow personal belongings. Since there was no electricity in the village, each of us was also equipped with a kerosene lantern, a box of matches, and a flashlight.

When I emerged after unpacking, I found Mariam already drawing water for my bath, using a much-knotted rope to lower a black plastic sack, shaped like a sheep's stomach, about twenty-five feet down into the well and then pouring this water into a green plastic pail. She seemed taken aback when I tried to help her and insisted on drawing the water and carrying the bucket to the latrine herself; I followed with my bar of soap and my red Cannon bath towel.

The latrine was primitive but functional—a walled area with a six-inch hole in the center of a cement platform and another drain off to one side to carry the used washwater out to the courtyard where it made a red-brown puddle for the family's two ducks to wallow in. I scrubbed up in the water-saving way we'd been taught.

In the evening after a communal meal with my fellow volunteers, I returned to the compound to find all the Keitas had reassembled to continue their welcome. Handshaking and hand-holding are terribly important in this society, and when I later moved into Bamako, it took me quite a while to get used to the common sight of men walking down the street holding hands. All evening, various Keitas kept taking my hand, or my wrist if the hand was taken, and some of the smaller children grasped me by a pant leg. A few of the tiniest seemed frightened by the presence of a husky, white-maned *tubab* and hid behind their mothers and whimpered when I approached to reassure them.

Once I had been properly greeted for the second time, the family began enthusiastically to teach me the Bambara words for every object they could point at. In less than an hour I had recorded in my notebook the native words (as nearly as I could spell them) for millet, mortar, pestle, hoe, water, mango, mango leaf, fishnet, mat, bowl, spoon, latrine, and so many other useful and useless words and expressions that I despaired of learning any of them. They were almost all nouns—hardly any verbs at all except such easily-mimicked ones as "eat," "sleep," and "sit," and no prepositions, adverbs, or other kinds of grammatical glue that might have helped me put them into phrases. At about eleven o'clock, I excused myself in pantomime and tumbled exhausted into bed.

According to old habit, I woke with the first glimmer of day. The local muezzin was beginning his call to prayer, and cocks were crowing and donkeys hee-hawing all over the village. In the courtyard, Mariam was tending her cooking fire, and in the half-dark street outside, I could just make out the shapes of women pounding millet in great wooden mortars; soon I saw the forms of men moving off with their short-handled hoes to the fields or with their nets to the river. Apparently old Birama had left even before this, for at about 6:30, as I was leaving to join my fellow volunteers for morning bread and coffee, he returned proudly with a large iguana-like creature in his net. He explained in sign language that it was good to eat.

It didn't take me long to discover that privacy would be a rarity. Each evening when I came home at nine or ten o'clock, exhausted by a day of classes in the 100-plus-degree heat, I would find my "family" waiting eagerly for me and, within minutes, all the relatives would arrive to try once again my fluency in Bambara. During those first days, conversation was a nearly hopeless task despite their brave efforts, and after an hour or so I would excuse myself as politely as I could and take a bucket of water out to the open-air latrine for a bath, then head for bed.

This didn't always assure peace. Family and friends continued to hang out on the other side of my screen door and to wake me from time to time with questions and incomprehensible comments. One evening I was called from bed to chat with a dozen young women and children who were outside in the street pounding a nutlike fruit called *cbi* to make oil for cooking. They seemed excited to discover I was unmarried and immediately began a game of matchmaking. Soon I found myself the object of the aggressive attentions of a pretty fourteen-year-old girl who hoped to enter a Bamako lycée in the fall and would be studying English there. I escaped by making believe it was all a friendly joke, and probably to some extent it was, but I was beginning to suspect that this was not going to be the last of such attentions: I might have been sixty-six years old, with a current income of barely $25 a week, but by Malian standards I was apparently a live prospect for marriage.

While I and my fellow volunteers were soaking up the environment, the serious business of training continued—training in our duties, in the local culture, and especially in languages. In twelve weeks, we would be scattered all over the country, the majority alone in remote villages where their English would be totally useless and they would have to communicate in Bambara with the villagers they worked with, and in French with the Malian officials who supervised them. None of us, of course, knew Bambara, and only a few knew French well enough to actually use it; shockingly, some had passed all the way through high school and college in America without having once attempted a foreign language of any kind, and for these the difficulties were almost overwhelming.

Except for Monica, the snub-nosed Irish-American who had been flown over from the States, all our instructors were Malians—lycée teachers on vacation or graduate students of education at the normal school where I would soon be teaching. We met in small groups of three or four of roughly the same level, and from eight each morning until noon we studied both Bambara and French; English was allowed only at breakfast and in the evening.

Lunch was another training exercise: We had to get used to making rice the central part of the meal as the Malians do, rather than treating it as a side dish. It didn't take us long to discover that a bowl of rice and sauce was far less filling than an equivalent portion of meat and potatoes. Fortunately, there were always seconds for the volunteers. After lunch and siesta, classes continued until six, and often resumed for a couple of hours after dinner, which was usually cooked and served American-style.

Fishing with Birama

On weekends, our heavy training schedule was relaxed so we could spend time with our families. This usually meant working in the fields with them, because summer—the rainy season—is the height of the growing period and everyone—man, woman, and child—spends the days in the fields, cultivating millet with short-handled hoes called *dabas*. They wield these close to the ground with one hand and, unbelievably, never bend their knees; their working posture reminded me of Van Gogh's "The Potato Eaters," and I wasn't surprised to learn that low-back problems are common among elderly people in Mali.

Birama was too feeble to be of much use as a cultivator, but usually fished instead. One fine Friday evening, I asked if I could join him the next morning, and he was as delighted as a child.

Serious fishing in Moribabougou is done not with rod and line, but with a casting net. The traditional net is conical, about eight feet across at the open end, which is weighted with lead around its circumference. The idea, Birama demonstrated, was to gather the narrow, closed end in folds with the left hand where it is secured to the wrist with a cord, and then to spread the open end between the right hand and the teeth. This done, the fisherman makes a kind of two-handed Frisbee toss, letting go with teeth and hands at precisely the right moment. If he does this correctly, the spinning mouth of the net will open full and circular, and the whole thing will then sail gracefully through the air to land evenly on the water fifteen to twenty feet away.

15

I practiced this a few times that evening, mostly without success, and the next morning we headed for the river.

At Moribabougou, the Niger flows through or over a kind of plain of black basaltic rock. We followed a small branch that eons ago had eroded a course through the softer places in the stone, making its narrow way roughly parallel to the main river before rejoining it a few miles downstream. It was like a succession of small pools joined by streams that barely moved. We stopped at one of these pools, and Birama stripped off his shirt, trousers, and sandals, and waded into the water, looking thin and boyish in the western-style shorts he'd been wearing underneath. His first cast was a weak one, and he ducked beneath the surface to free the net from rocks and weeds.

Now it was my turn. I stripped to my jockey shorts, took the net firmly in teeth and hands, waded into the stream, and cast. Alas, I was so fearful of being yanked into the water by my dentures that I let go of everything much too soon, and the whole net, weights and all, splashed at my feet in a noisy clump. Impossible to fish that hole again, so we pushed on. As the day wore on, I learned to make a halfway decent cast, but neither of us caught a fish.

Back home, Mariam was waiting with a dinner of rice and sauce and was unhappy with us both for bringing her no fish to cook with it.

A Visit to the Family Chief

On my second weekend in Moribabougou, there were no classes and Mariam reminded me that it was high time I paid a courtesy call on old Balamine Keita, the chief of all the Keitas in Moribabougou. From outside, Balamine's mud-walled compound looked much like Birama's across the lane, except a bit bigger, but inside the old man's affluence was immediately apparent: there were animals everywhere. A donkey—probably the same donkey that had been waking me every morning—was munching leaves near the entrance, and tethered a few feet away stood a skinny brown cow. A small black goat and a pair of husky-looking rams were browsing on cut branches near what I took to be a latrine, and chickens, ducks, and small children were everywhere. One of these last was my erstwhile helper, Idrissa. Mariam turned me over to Fatoumata, Balamine's number-one wife, and she in turn presented me to her husband.

I recognized Balamine immediately as one of the elders who had welcomed us to the village. He was a massive, white-bearded man, a quiet center of power and unquestioned authority, and he received me regally on his verandah, seated cross-legged on a bamboo cot. Shrugging off my futile efforts to talk with him in Bambara, he waved me to a stool and insisted on conducting our conversation in French, which he had learned in the French army while fighting across North Africa during World War II, and later while he was for six years a prisoner in Vietnam after the great French defeat at Dien Bien Phu.

He asked my age and, when I told him I'd just turned sixty-six, he smiled benignly and told me he was eighty-five and the father of Birama and all the other middle-aged and elderly-looking Keitas in the village. He then called over a youngish woman who was nursing a child and introduced her as his latest wife and the baby as his daughter. He chortled pridefully at this demonstration of his continuing vigor and, after he had translated his remarks into Bambara, the onlooking wives and children laughed loudly. Fatoumata, the jolly, strapping number-one wife who had met me when I entered, dashed into one of the rooms off the verandah and returned with another woman who was identified to me as the second of Balamine's three wives. She was clearly five or six months pregnant, and her eyes gleamed with pleasure as the old man patted her swollen belly.

"You'll have to find yourself a wife while you're here," he said. "It is not good for an old man to live alone."

A Family Intrigue

Balamine kept needling me about women and I began to suspect he was trying to arrange something. One day he mentioned several young girls in his family who would be happy to have an American husband. Since our Peace Corps training hadn't yet prepared me for this particular kind of cultural immersion, I got by as best I could by retreating into honesty.

"Balamine," I told him, "I'm an intellectual. I need a woman who can talk with me, not just cook and keep me warm in bed. I would not be happy long with an uneducated girl."

This turned out to be the right way to talk to the old man, for it apparently wakened some memory from his army days of French officers who read books and wrote letters. "I know someone for you," he said. "She was once married to a European and she has only one child, a very light-skinned boy. She knows how to talk with a white man."

"But how can I take a wife, Balamine?" I asked. "In two years my service will be over and I will have to leave here and go back to America." He dismissed this obstacle with a kingly wave.

"When you go back to America, you can divorce her. Then every month you can send her a little money for the children."

The children. Well.

The weekend after this intriguing conference with Balamine, two new faces appeared in my parents' compound: a plain, sad-eyed young woman

17

(divorcee? widow?) named Sofiatou and her five- or-six-year-old son Madou, a light-skinned boy, partly European, I was sure. Within half an hour of his arrival, Madou was following me around as affectionately as if I were his father.

Dear, dear Balamine. He was a complex man but a very simple one. I first suspected that he was just hoping to find a safe landing place for one of the surplus females in his family, but I realize now that he was also befriending me in his fashion and I think I know why. We were members of the same club.

Of all the bonds that tie people to one another in this ancient culture—kin to kin, tribe to tribe, husband to wife, and generation to generation—blood kinship is certainly the strongest. Close behind this, though, is the sacred bond of age, especially among men. Old men here are brothers, members of an elite and imperiled society open only to those who have paid the full price of experience and suffering. And, because they have survived, these old men are the unquestioned repositories of power and, presumably, of wisdom as well. My sex, white hair, and weathered face had earned me automatic membership in this club, and my skin color seemed to make very little difference.

I Am Introduced to Islam

From sunup to sundown, seven days a week, work is the pattern of life in villages like Moribabougou, interrupted in summer only by frequent short and heavy rains. Friday afternoon, though, is special because it is the Sabbath, the holy day, and all the men of the village go to the mosque to pray. Some of the more devout women go as well but are segregated in a special section—"the back of the bus," as one female volunteer called it. One Friday morning at about eleven, I was on my way to the river to take pictures when the village's pint-sized local reverend, the imam, stopped me and insisted that I come into the mosque and join the other men in their prayers. I was nervous about accepting, for fear I might accidentally do some uncouth thing, the religious equivalent of dipping my left hand into the communal bowl, but I was curious and flattered and didn't want to appear disrespectful, so I agreed.

Islam crossed the Sahara into the great hump of West Africa with Arab merchants and scholars as early as the seventh century. The local kings and tribal chiefs found that trade was easier and more profitable when they adopted some, at least, of these strangers' ways, and soon Islam was the nominal religion in the courts and among the wealthier classes in cities like Audagast, Kumbeh Saleh, and Timbuktoo. It was a fairly relaxed form of Islam, adopted less from conviction than for expediency, and the majority of the common people stayed true to their ancient gods. Ibn Batuta, an Arab traveler of the fourteenth century, complained that he couldn't go to the mosque in Timbuktoo for prayers without being jostled on his way by dozens of naked serving girls coming from the market. Over the years, Islam penetrated deeper, and today, about 80 percent of the population of Mali is said to be Muslim. Of the rest, about 10 percent are Christian, and the declining remainder are animist. There was a surge of rigid fundamentalism among West African Moslems during the nineteenth century, but for most devout believers in Mali, Islam is still a fairly comfortable religion.

At the entrance to the mosque, the imam slipped his feet gracefully out of his *jalabas*, the sharp-toed, open-heeled slippers orthodox Moslems wear for just that purpose, and gestured for me to do likewise. I was wearing laced-up running shoes with thick athletic socks. Clumsily, I took them off and placed them by the row of jalabas, sandals, and plastic flip-flops next to the door and followed the imam inside.

This was the regular Friday morning service, but there was no sermon, no music as in the churches I'd been used to in America, just a succession of prayers in Arabic, which scarcely anyone in the village seemed to understand, but which everyone had memorized well enough to chant in unison. I understood nothing, of course, but I did my best to keep up with the acrobatic movements of the congregation, alternately standing, kneeling, kneeling prostrate, and sitting cross-legged in a kind of lotus position. When the service was over, I was almost crippled, but everyone smiled at me and nobody laughed. Then the imam led me to his house to take pictures of his three wives, and insisted on a present of fifty francs for each.

When I told Balamine about this later, he was embarrassed. "Our imam is famous for his greed," he said.

19

3

Born Again

F ive weeks after my arrival in the village, I was officially inducted into the Keita family at a mass "baptism," or togo da, held in the school playground. It was a momentous evening. When I arrived, shortly after nightfall, half a dozen drummers were loosening up on their tom-toms by the light of a small fire. Around them and perhaps fifty yards away, several hundred chairs had been arranged in a circle; these were intended for us celebrants and our families but were under attack all evening by hordes of small children who were periodically chased away by schoolteachers wielding small, leafy branches. Little by little, the edges of the schoolyard began to fill up as clusters of villagers with flashlights and kerosene lanterns streamed in like fireflies. They stood behind us, many holding children above their heads.

Sometime about ten-thirty, the bonfire was stoked and the drummers began beating out a chain of those African rhythms so difficult to imitate and so impossible to sit still to. One of my relatives by marriage, John Chernoff, spent eight years in West Africa studying drum music and wrote a fascinating book about it. His thesis, as I understand it, is that Africans invest in their rhythms the same degree of complexity that Europeans invest in their harmonies, and that an "orchestra" of tom-toms—each drum of a designated shape and size and tuned to a different pitch and timbre—plays a rhythmic counterpoint every bit as intricate as the tonal counterpoint in a Bach fugue.

Whatever the case, it's not music to sleep by, and within minutes almost every Malian at the baptismal party, whether he or she could dance or not, had moved into the ring and begun sashaying about in what I supposed to be a kind of traditional pattern, the men circling the women who were clapping hands and moving forward and back in a smaller circle within. Every so often, some individual dancer or pair of dancers would catch fire and move to the center for a few moments of furious acrobatics, then move out so another could take his turn. These star acts stirred the tom-toms to new heights of enthusiasm and, by the time the big moment arrived, all were outwardly and inwardly jumping. I was comforted to see that not everyone danced well.

The signal for the ceremonies to begin was a blast on a police whistle by Ibrahim Traorè, the school principal. Immediately, the tom-toms quieted, a generator was cranked up, and a string of five or six naked light bulbs illuminated a microphone in the center of the ring of chairs. One by one, each host family was called to the front with the volunteer living with them. An African name was formally bestowed, the tom-toms beat a crescendo, and the crowd cheered. The first few families to take the spotlight were a bit stiff, but the drumming began to get to everyone and, as everywhere, there turned out to be showboats among both the Malians and the Peace Corps Volunteers. Soon, no name-giving was complete without an impromptu dance, some quite spectacular.

Alas, when my family's turn came, it was Sofiatou, not Mariam and Birama, who did the honors. They had stayed home, pleading fatigue (although, as it turned out, there were other reasons) and had sent Sofiatou and little Madou in their place. She was magnificently robed for the affair, wearing an apparently brand-new *boubou* of gold *bazin* (a kind of shiny damask cloth) and her hair was intricately braided with black thread and blue and gold beads. Madou wore a new boubou as well. On the opposite side of the ring, I saw my young porter Idrissa waving frantically as if he had some urgent secret to share.

At a signal from the master of ceremonies, Sofiatou muttered my new name out of hearing of the microphone and had to repeat it three times before it was audible, even to me: "Namory." Now a great roar did indeed burst out. The tom-toms renewed their insistent beat, and at that moment I knew I was not simply being named but was actually being initiated into a new way of perceiving the world and responding to it.

My dance, friends told me later, was memorable—and courageous. The courage probably came from my understanding that African dances are

21

not so much performances as they are kinds of invocation or ritualized storytelling, and that my good intentions might therefore atone for my lack of grace. I prefer to think, however, that weeks of primitive living and insistent tom-tomming had stirred some subliminal memory in my genes. No matter. The stiffness, the self-consciousness, the sheer inability to feel in my bones the beat of the music that had kept me on the sidelines at every school dance I attended, from junior high on—all these simply dropped away.

I began, apparently, with two complete circles of the ring at full gallop, clapping my hands and punctuating my savage race every twenty or thirty feet or so with reckless leaps into the crowd; strong hands caught me every time. By then thoroughly in the mood I improvised a little story—an old man successively wooing, winning, and naughtily enjoying each of the four wives permitted him by the Qur'an, wrenching his back four times in the process, finally falling exhausted and writhing to the ground. There are moments that we know, even while we are living them, can never be approached again, and this was such a one.

It must have been after two a.m. when we left for home—Sofiatou with the lamp leading the way and myself following with the sleeping Madou cradled in my arms. Mariam and Birama were up waiting for us and, for half an hour or so, various Keitas kept dropping in out of the darkness to welcome me into the family. Finally the last well-wisher left, Madou was put to bed, and I was left with Birama, Mariam, and my twenty-five-year-old proxy-parent, Sofiatou—"the family."

We chatted for half an hour or so in our now habitual combination of sign language and pigeon Bambara. Mariam, it seems, had indeed come to the affair while Birama napped, and was impressed by my "vigor," I think she called it. Sofiatou, who knows a little French, translated this. "You have much force for an old man."

And suddenly I came to realize that nothing that had happened to me that week, nothing that was happening to me now, was accidental. Balamine's little chats, Sofiatou's arrival, Madou's lovably easy identification with me as a kind of substitute father, and, tonight, Mariam and Birama's abdication of parenthood in favor of the boy's spectacularly coiffured young mother—all were parts of a design. Madam spun the homely Sofiatou slowly around like a mannequin on a turntable, pointing out each feature of her dress, each braid in her coiffure.

"Is she not beautiful?"

A lovely and terrible moment. Every dram of self-assurance the tom-toms had drummed into me drizzled out of my pores in a cold sweat. "Yes, she is beautiful."

Long pause. Actually, an embarrassed pause, its nature hardly concealed by our habitual difficulties with language. It was hard not to know what was going on.

Most Malian women are not one bit assertive, especially before men. Mariam is an exception. She is an activist. She put her hand on my shoulder, pointed unmistakably to the double bed in the room she and Birama shared, and repeated, "Isn't she beautiful?"

I muttered something that I cannot remember, and Mariam gave us both a gentle push toward the bedroom. "Sleep," she said.

I've never had trustworthy gut responses. As a teenager, I always discovered the bright riposte minutes after the occasion for it had passed, and would sometimes spend an entire evening trying to return the conversation to a point where I could astound everyone with my prepared witticism. But this time, what? Any other red-blooded American male—hell, any red-blooded African male, almost any male at all—would have swept the willing and waiting Sophiatou across the threshold and done what nature, prolonged abstinence, and his new parents were commanding, then worried the next day about consequences.

Not I. Consequences were all I could think about. Would a night in the sack with Sophiatou—especially such a well-orchestrated night—be the cultural equivalent of marriage? Would I then be responsible for her? For Madou? What would happen when I left the village after my training? When I returned in two years to the U.S.?

But then, what would be the implications of saying no? Would my semi-public rejection of Sophiatou be seen as an unforgivable insult to her? To my new parents? To Balamine? To the entire Keita clan to which she belonged? Cowardice gripped me with its chilly claws, and I knew that whatever brave spontaneity I had felt during my baptismal dance was a lie. "N'ma famu," I stammered. "I don't understand. I don't understand."

Mariam became more explicit, almost pornographic, in her pantomimes.

"N'ma famu. I don't understand," I repeated helplessly, and scurried to the safety of my room. Not an auspicious way to begin a reincarnation.

My New Ancestors

The week following the mass name-day was a quiet one, for all the new rural volunteers had taken off for experimental "live-ins"—sharing for a week the work and lifestyles of their more seasoned counterparts in "the bush," as the countryside is called. Only we seven new English teachers were left behind. I spent the time learning more about my new name.

23

It seems I had been inducted into one of the most illustrious families in West Africa. Some 750 years ago, "twenty years after the signing of the Magna Charta in England" according to the Peace Corps' *Mali Handbook*, a young man named Sundiata Keita led his Mandinke tribesmen in revolt against the ruling Tekrurs. He defeated them on a plain just north of present-day Bamako, and went on to found one of the greatest empires in human history. At its zenith in the fourteenth century, the Empire of Mali was about the size of western Europe today and stretched from the Atlantic Ocean in the west almost to present-day Chad in the east, and from the dry Sahara in the north to the rain forests far to the south.

Sundiata made his capital in his hometown of Niani, near the rich gold fields of Wangaba, but the commercial and intellectual heart of the Empire was the legendary city of Timbuktoo. From here, the Keitas dominated the trans-Saharan trade routes in salt, gold, ivory, and slaves for over three hundred years.

My regal ancestors lived in imperial style and established an extraordinary reputation for opulence. "The lord of this kingdom," a Moroccan traveler wrote in the fourteenth century, "has a great seat of ebony that is like a throne for a large and tall person. It is flanked by elephants' tusks. The king's arms . . . are all of gold; sword and lance, quiver of bow and arrows. He wears wide trousers made of twenty pieces of stuff, and they are of a kind which he alone may wear. Before him stand about twenty Turkish or other pages, who are brought from Cairo. One of these, standing on his left, holds a silk umbrella that is topped by a bird and dome of gold. The bird is like a hawk. The king's officers are seated in a circle near him. Beyond them sit the commanders of the cavalry. In front of him there is a person who never leaves him and who is his executioner; and another who is his official spokesman, and who is named herald. In front of him there are also drummers . . . Others dance before the king and make him merry."

One of the best known of my imperial ancestors was Mansa Musa Keita who, in 1324, made a pilgrimage to Mecca where he gave away tons—*literally* tons—of gold to the poor; his generosity so flooded the area with gold that the monetary systems of the Middle East, and especially of Egypt, were said to be in chaos for years afterward. Musa's largesse was not without return. When he left Mecca, he brought with him to the ancient trading center of Timbuktoo a vast library of religious, scientific, and historical works and enough Arabic scholars to transform the city into one of the most famous centers of learning in the late Middle Ages.

Namory was one of the great leaders of the Keita clan, but he is remembered more for his wisdom than for his freespending or his leadership in battle. He was, explained Balamine, a *marabout*, a wise and holy man with gifts of healing and prophecy; Mariam pictured him in sign language by shading her eyes with her right hand and looking off into the distance, in the manner of Tonto, the Indian scout.

Namory, which means "big Mory," was also the name of Balamine's father, the founder of Moribabougou. It was the old man himself who chose the name for me, and I knew I had been significantly honored.

4

Making a Home
in the City

My aging knees never did take kindly to squatting over a hole in the concrete, and one dark night when I was suffering my lone attack of diarrhea during all my years in Mali, I missed the hole altogether and spent an hour cleaning up the mess by flashlight. Still, I was not happy when, the summer not two-thirds over, the English teachers in our group were pulled out of the rude but peaceful culture of Moribabougou and plunged into the hurly-burly of Bamako—a capital city of nearly a million people (it has grown since) with open sewers and not a single well-paved street.

Here there were no tom-toms to celebrate our arrival, no families prepared to welcome us as sons and daughters. We had each to scour the city for our own lodgings, finding our way as best we could in makeshift Bambara. (French was sometimes of help, but English was of no use whatever.) Barely two weeks before the opening of school, I found the home I was looking for.

It wasn't much by expatriate standards—a shabby, three-room, concrete villa in the "industrial" zone (a designation more indicative of hope than of reality since there was still virtually no industry in Bamako), just a few streets from the Peace Corps' mimeograph machine, which I had been warned I

26

would use often because of the shortage of books at the school. The painted walls were stained, the tile floors were chipped, the lighting glared from overhead fluorescent fixtures, but the little house was set in a small walled courtyard dominated by three enormous mango trees. Mangoes have a spreading growth habit something like our maples, and I would not only have fresh fruit during the dry season, but cooling shade all year round. I used the bargaining skills taught me in Moribabougou to negotiate with a street-corner craftsman for twelve pieces of handmade bamboo furniture at a total cost of less than $135 American and bought a beat-up gas stove and a bottle of gas for about $75 more. I was at home in Africa.

Life with my poor family in Moribabougou had in no way prepared me for the really grinding poverty I found in Bamako, less than an hour away. I'd hardly been in the city a week when it became sharply clear that the struggle to keep alive my own sense of well-being amidst the abject misery of so many others was going to be an inescapable theme of my life for the next two years.

Miriam and Birama were poor, yes; they lived without electricity or running water in a little house of mud and cement block; their diet was almost entirely rice, with occasional scraps of meat or fish; and for a latrine they had only a walled hole in a cement slab. They were, in fact, one of the poorest families in that very poor village, for they were childless and Birama was too old and feeble to cultivate his field without help. Yet blood ties are strong in Mali, and Miriam and Birama were never without companionship or dignity, and never allowed to go hungry. Living with them, I never felt we were truly "poor."

In Bamako, on the other hand, the evidences of poverty were overwhelming. I noticed them first in the decaying government buildings, almost all built during the French colonial period, which ended in 1960, in the shabby, tin-roofed stores, in the unpaved streets, and in the filthy open sewers. But what really brought it home to me was the visible penury of the people themselves.

Bamako had a population of nearly a million but there was no private industry whatever and only the most rudimentary commerce. The nation's only substantial employer was the government, and this was itself so poor and so corrupt that civil servants seldom got their pay until three months or more after it was due. For a few lucky others, there were domestic positions as houseboys, watchmen, or laundresses for the foreigners here, and for those both lucky and educated, there was a coveted handful of positions in banks, missions, and international organizations. The vast majority of the population, marginally literate and with no luck at all, fended for itself or depended on the traditional and unflagging hospitality of relatives. As might be expected, theft was commonplace.

Even the few well-to-do Malians and members of the European community could hardly escape the oppressive omnipresence of poverty as they rode in air-conditioned cars from their well-kept suburban villas to shop for clothes, wine, and choice meats in the center of town. The roadsides were dotted, the sidewalks crowded with men at rickety tables and women squatting beside hollowed calabash gourds, selling flashlight batteries, cigarettes (one or two at a time), tea and sugar (the standard measure was a shot glass), fruits, vegetables, and cooked snacks—whatever could be made by hand or bought on credit or consignment and sold at a tiny profit. Some sellers carried their entire inventories on their heads—watches, cassette tapes, household tools, bolts of printed cloth; many took home less than a dollar for twelve hours of work. And everywhere hordes of importunate children were demanding five or six cents for a plastic bag in which to carry home the merchandise.

Lining the streets and roads into the city center, hundreds of small artisans waited patiently by their benches and stands, ready to make or mend clothes, fix watches, resole shoes, or repair eyeglasses for just enough to salvage self-respect. Near the Peace Corps office, repairers had stationed themselves and their pitiful stores of tools on nearly every corner, waiting patiently for a bicycle, mobylette, or motorcycle to break down so they could fix it by the side of the road. The going price for repairing a bicycle tire was about three cents per puncture.

The common people of West Africa have been coping with poverty for centuries, in city and in country, and those who have retained the capacity to struggle seem neither embittered nor ashamed, so their visible miseries aren't really depressing. Far more difficult for me to deal with were the multitudinous beggars. These were everywhere, or seemed to be, but they were especially plentiful at the market and at the entrances to the mosques—ragged boys and girls with small tin pails, kept out of school to beg rice for the family meal; adult victims of childhood paralysis, with legs like toothpicks and shoulders like Hercules' from dragging themselves about the streets by hands and arms; old men, formerly fishermen or riverbank farmers, blinded by fly-borne parasites and now led about by children at the ends of bamboo poles; red-eyed lepers as frightening as tales from the Bible, missing fingers, toes, hands, feet, even portions of their noses and ears.

At first, I tried to avoid looking at any of these unfortunates, and I stayed away as often as I could from the mosques and bazaars where they congregated. I wasn't being cheap. I was trying to avoid discomfort, and confrontation with such gross suffering and disfigurement made me feel unbearably guilty. Then one day, coming out of Malimag, the city's only "department store," I noticed a well-dressed, well-nourished African ahead of me walk past a line of beggars and carefully, almost ceremoniously, present a small coin to each. I talked about this later with a Malian friend, and he explained that every Muslim favored with good fortune is expected to share a little of it with those who were not. Ten or twenty francs—one or two cents—was the usual offering.

From this moment, I began to make a point of carrying a supply of these small coins with me and pausing to give one, with the traditional greeting, to every beggar I passed. This led me to look at each of these unfortunates as an individual, and I soon realized that there weren't really quite so many of them as I had imagined when they were anonymous—not at all as in the movies of India—just a large, but still countable number of very unlucky people.

One of these unfortunates was a middle-aged leper woman who spent her daytime hours alternately squatting and sleeping on the raised sidewalk by the entrance to the state bank where I cashed my checks. She was an apparition—her nose half eaten away, her hair disheveled, her lips and tongue stained henna-orange from her addiction to cola nuts. Coming out of the bank one day, I put my twenty-franc offering in her tin can, murmuring the Islamic blessing I had been taught for such occasions. Then, for reasons I cannot understand, I took her fingerless right hand in mine and spoke to her in the traditional Malian manner of greeting a friend. What a radiant response this easy gesture earned! She told me her name was Hawa.

El Haji

My landlord, El Haji Boundy Gassouma, called by everyone just "El Haji," a title of respect bestowed on Muslim men who have made the pilgrimage to Mecca, was a shrewd-looking man with a long, sharp nose, small, darting eyes, and a wispy gray beard on his pointed chin; when he talked business, his hands flickered excitedly, like long black flames.

Most of the ethnic groups in Mali traditionally follow a single occupation—the Bambaras farming, the Fulanis herding, the Bozos fishing, and so on. El Haji belonged to the ethnic group called "Saracole," who are merchants. Unlike members of the other ethnic groups who (except for the nomads in the north) cling as if glued to their native places, the Saracole seem to have little attachment to home, or at least to place, and freely pick up stakes to go wherever business is good. El Haji had three wives, one for when he had business in Senegal, one for when he traveled to Ivory Coast, and one here in Bamako. Unlike most Malians, El Haji never bothered with the tradi-

29

tional polite salutations, but plunged right into the money matters at hand. In appearance and personality, he would have been perfectly cast as a dark-skinned Shylock.

Fanta

I see I have written unkindly of El Haji, and in truth he was an austere, grasping, unsympathetic man. But he did one very good thing for me. He introduced me to Fanta.

Fanta and her nine-year-old granddaughter Ami ("lent" to Fanta by her mother in the same way that Modibo had been lent by his parents to Mariam and Birama) shared a one-room house in the yard of El Haji's warehouse next door. For the equivalent of seventy-five cents a day, old Fanta, who is now a great-grandmother many times over, agreed to bring me a hearty lunch each noon and to keep my courtyard and the street in front of my house neatly swept of fallen leaves. For another $20 a month, I also engaged Fanta's daughter Aminata, who is Ami's mother, to do my laundry and part-time housekeeping. She arrived each morning at seven towing Ami's five-year-old sister Madinè by the hand and carrying her two-year-old brother Badara swaddled on her back. I didn't know it then, but I had acquired another family.

Fanta, it turned out, was a gifted cook and, even though each meal was mostly rice with two or three bites of meat and occasionally a vegetable thrown in, I never tasted the same dish twice. Sometimes the sauce was garlicky, sometimes highly peppered or thickened with okra. Occasionally the basic onion-tomato sauce was replaced by one flavored with peanut butter or dried fish, and once in a while Fanta cooked millet or couscous instead of rice. Every meal was a surprise and there was always enough to go round when friends dropped by unexpectedly, or for me to reheat with curry powder or some other change of seasoning for dinner.

Early one morning shortly after I had settled in, Fanta arrived at my door bearing on her head a carton of cuttings that she had apparently scrounged from neighbors' gardens. She insisted I plant them in my barren courtyard then and there, pointing wordlessly where each naked stick must go, then standing by while I installed it. Two or three days later, she brought more. I hadn't the faintest idea what any of these sticks were, nor did I know how to ask, but I took the short-handled hoe, or *daba*, Fanta handed me and planted them anyway.

Planting, of course, was just the beginning. The last rain of the year had fallen in mid-September and there wouldn't be another until June, so gardening meant watering every morning and watering every night. Fanta took the early shift and I took the late one. For the next three months, until I finally broke down and bought a hose, I was gently wakened at six o'clock each morning by the sound of old Fanta irrigating my bare sticks from a pail.

Kadia

Fanta prepared my lunches, the big meal of the day, but I did most of my own cooking in the evening, and Fanta's friend Kadia would stop by in the late afternoon to sell me vegetables. I'm not good at guessing the ages of Malian women: In their twenties, they look younger than they actually are; later, they look older. Kadia was probably in her early forties, fine-boned and lean like most Fulanis, the shepherd people of West Africa, with an aristocratic neck and a long, narrow nose—a darker version of the women in Gainsborough's paintings. If Kadia had not been missing two of her front teeth, she would have been truly beautiful.

Kadia struck me as exceptionally tall, but this might have been because I seldom saw her without a great nest of calabashes balanced on her head, each containing kilos of the freshest vegetables one could find in Bamako. I knew how heavy they were, because I had to help lift them off her head when she arrived and lift them back up when she left.

In addition to the merchandise on her head, Kadia always carried her youngest child on her back like Aminata, swaddled in a bandana-size kerchief tied around her breasts and waist. She peddled her vegetables from about seven in the morning until after eight or sometimes nine in the evening, going from house to house throughout the neighborhood. Sometimes she was accompanied by two other of her children, a boy I supposed to be about seven and a girl a bit younger. They each carried something, the little boy almost as much as his mother, and they did this with no apparent complaint. On several occasions when Kadia's lower back was bothering her, she would lie down on the paving stones while the boy jumped up and down on her spine.

Like most Malian families, Kadia's was polygamous. Polygamy is declining somewhat among the middle and professional classes here in Bamako, but it is still widely practiced in the countryside for it permits enormous families and thus provides many hands to work the fields. (Shortly after I started teaching, one of my women students startled me with a composition entitled, "How My Father's Four Wives Made Him Rich.") Many farm women still say they like polygamy, because it spreads their work around.

And surely there is always plenty of that.

In Moribagougou I could hear the women before daybreak pounding millet in great wooden mortars, and again in the evening after supper. They walked miles scavenging for firewood. which was becoming desperately scarce; they cooked and laundered for families of fifteen or twenty, sometimes more; they were almost always either pregnant or nursing; and, when all their "woman's work" was done, they were expected to be in the fields helping their husbands and sons. Another wife in the family was not necessarily a threat, but welcome help with the chores and, for many, relief from the husband's bed. They could now take turns visiting him in his room, two consecutive nights apiece.

Ami

Life in my new home soon fell into a comfortable routine. At six in the morning, I would be wakened by the scraping sound of Fanta's bundle of broom straws as she swept the leaves from the courtyard. This would remind me to put the coffee water on and to bike to the comer *boulangerie* for fresh-baked French bread, returning just as the water was coming to a boil. Fanta and little Ami would carry three bamboo chairs from the house into the court-yard where we would sit the for our ritual breakfast *en famille*—coffee, with bread and jam. I say "coffee," but Fanta and Ami, like the Malians I had met upon my arrival, and like most Malians, liked only a pinch of Nescafe in their hot water, plus a sickening quantity of *lait sucré*, the sweetened condensed milk that serves here as cream.

At 7:15 Ami would set off on her two-kilometer walk to school, and at 8:45 her mother Aminata would arrive to do the laundry, Ami's five-year-old sister Madinè trotting beside her and a two-year-old boy strapped to her back. During the next six months, I never saw Aminata take the baby down except to nurse him or to change him; all morning little Badara would ride piggyback right through the mopping and the wash. After more coffee, I would bike off to teach my classes and Aminata would water the garden with the hose.

Some months after settling in, I began a couple of correspondence chess games with my old friend Dick Gardner in New Jersey, and during the Christmas holidays I discovered that little Ami was following the moves I was making on the board. Already she had taught herself—just by watching—the placement of the pieces and the different ways they moved. She liked setting up the chessboard for me, and I showed her how the various pieces captured each other. Alas, with our near-total language barrier, that was as far as I could go, for I couldn't figure out how to explain to Ami that the object of the game was not just to capture my pieces, which she did with great zeal, but to trap my king, to checkmate me.

Ami loved playing anyway, and I was so enthralled by the energy and intelligence this nine-year-old brought to the game that we sometimes carried on at the chessboard for an hour or more with no hope either of us could win by conventional means.

If Ami had been enrolled in the regular public school, we'd have had no communications problem, for she would have been in the third grade and doing all her studies in French. However, many Malian parents feared (they still do) that western style schooling in reading, writing, and arithmetic might turn their daughters away from traditional ways, might corrupt them. Ami's father had decided that she should receive a religious education and had enrolled her in an Islamic, or "Franco-Arab," school where all instruction for the first three years is in Arabic. Only in the fourth grade would Ami begin the study of French, which is the official national language of her country. Nonetheless, she adored her school and often showed me her notebook filled with Muslim prayers neatly lettered in Arabic and with gold and silver stars added by the teacher.

Each morning after breakfast, Ami would tie her books together with a cotton strap and walk cheerily to the school three kilometers away. One morning, though, I noticed that she hadn't left, but instead was hanging around my house helping her mother. When I asked why, Aminata explained that the Islamic school would no longer allow the little girl to attend because her father was behind in paying her school fees of one thousand francs a month. The public school would have been free. And so of course I took on the responsibility for Ami's Islamic schooling.

This little African girl's diligence in her Arabic studies and her intelligence and persistence at the chessboard mocked better than any textbook could the segregationists' phony claims of black inferiority.

Stereotypes

I have heard Americans claim they have trouble telling one black person from another. To them they are all just "blacks" or "Negroes," and when a newspaper reports a crime committed by someone identified as "black," the stereotype is reinforced and, of course, the prejudice.

But, as I was one evening to discover, Africans have their own stereotypes of "Europeans," as all whites, regardless of their origins, are called. It was after supper, and we teachers were returning to Bamako after an afternoon of language lessons when our American driver committed some kind of minor infraction and was stopped by police. As luck would have it, he had with him not a single piece of identification—no driver's license, no vehicle registration, not even a passport or ID card. This would have been bad news anywhere, and for a while it looked as though we'd be held up all evening, perhaps even have the car impounded. Fortunately, another Peace Corps vehicle was right behind us and its driver, after a fast consultation in English, sneaked his own papers to the driver of our own. The gendarme took several minutes to compare the pudgy, clean-shaven image in the photo with the lean and bearded actuality of the driver himself, saw that both faces were white, and concluded they must belong to the same person.

The Sacrifice

Autumn is an ideal time of year to be in West Africa. The summer rains have washed away the red dust that coats the vegetation for nine months of the year, and the hot winds of the dry season have not yet browned the landscape. Trees and shrubs shine greenly under cloudless skies and the illusion of fertility is everywhere. I decided to take advantage of the comfortable weather to ride my one-speed bike the fifteen kilometers to Moribabougou in order to celebrate the feast of Tabaski with the Keitas.

Tabaski, one of the two great holidays of the Muslim year, is sometimes called the "Feast of Abraham," for Mohammed proclaimed the day holy to commemorate Abraham's absolute submission to God in offering his son Ismael (Isaac, according to Old Testament theology) as a sacrifice and God's infinite mercy in substituting, at the last split second, a fatted ram for the trembling child. On Tabaski, each family, however poor, strains its budget to buy and kill a ram (more rarely a cock or a billygoat), and to share the meat with family and friends and, especially, with those more unfortunate.

In spite of the move to Bamako, the umbilical cord to my family in Moribabougou had not been completely severed, and during the late summer I had returned there most afternoons for classes in language and culture. Sofiatou was no longer in the village, but her place in the Keita household had been filled by an old blind aunt named Djinessira, so feeble that Mariam had to guide her to the latrine and back again, but otherwise all was the same. Two weeks before the holiday, I helped Birama with the purchase of a small ram.

As I turned my bike into the lane leading to Birama's compound on the eve of the feast, children rushed out of doorways and from behind mud walls to give me the "high five" I had taught them while I was living there and to follow me down the street as if this were Hamelin town. At Birama's, more children were lying in wait, Mariam was drawing water from the well, Birama was resting under the mango tree in the rope hammock I had given him when I lived there and which he carefully took in every night for fear of thieves. Tethered by the door to my old room stood a skinny, short-haired young ram, munching leaves and bleating miserably for his fellows.

I reserved my sentiments for Mariam and Birama, who seemed ecstatically content, and left to pay my obligatory respects to the other families of the

Keita clan, presenting each adult with the traditional house present of a cola nut, prized for its bitter flavor and the mild caffeine high it induces. My first call was on old Balamine. He had just returned from a pilgrimage to Mecca in a plane with other Malian Moslems who could afford a few hundred thousand francs each to ensure their safe arrival in Paradise. Balamine smiled broadly when I greeted him as "El Haji" and urged me to make the pilgrimage myself.

At cockcrow the next morning, Birama's brother Issa, who seems to be about the same age but is a lot sturdier, came over to help with the preparations. These began with a ritual cleansing of the victim. Mariam brought out a calabash filled with warm, sudsy water, and each of us three men was assigned a part of the creature to make clean for sacrifice. I was given the rear end and Issa the foreparts, so we could hold the animal still during the washing; Birama was assigned a token area around the middle. I had never scrubbed a ram before, and certainly not his cock, balls, and anus, but astonishingly the ritual character of what we were doing—my awareness that I was simply repeating a rite that had been performed over and over again since Genesis—kept my mind focused. The sacrificial ram made everything easier by appearing to enjoy the attention.

The animal clean, it was time to purify ourselves. Mariam brought out more soapy water, we men took turns in the latrine scrubbing up, and Birama lent me a worn-looking white robe to wear to the mosque. The whole village was there, men and women seated separately. Because of the crowd, the service could not be held inside, so everyone sat or squatted on mats in the courtyard, shoes and sandals laid neatly alongside. Again, I could not follow the words of the ceremony, but the actions were clear.

As the prayers were about to begin, I noticed that each man was going through a private exercise in concentration. This lasted about a minute, the entire congregation standing at a kind of rigid attention, hands pressed against sides, eyes staring to the front, completely silent. Concentration is always a striking phenomenon to observe: Here I was reminded of nothing more reverent than a horde of Olympic athletes psyching themselves up for a simultaneous triple somersault from the diving tower.

Eventually, a young bullock was led out by half a dozen elders, including Balamine, and, with a little help from one of the younger men, neatly thrown and tied. The elders crowded round the animal and, led by the imam, began a recitation from the Qur'an. Behind the wall of old men, nothing could be seen. Finally there was a pause in the prayers and the elders stepped back; the ritual sacrifice was complete. There were more prayers, in which I joined by pantomime, and everyone left for home.

Issa's knife, too, was mercifully sharp. He had dug a small depression in the earth of the courtyard, and together we laid the young ram gently on the ground, its throat just over the hollow. Again I held the rear legs while Issa held the head. Birama looked on. It was over in a moment, the blood gushing into the scooped-out earth and soaking quickly into it. The knife must have cut instantly through jugular, windpipe, and voicebox, for there was not a cry and hardly a tremor in the wooly body beneath my hands.

Immediately, Issa and Birama set to work to skin and eviscerate the carcass, giving Mariam and the two women helping her the stomach, intestines, and other precious innards to clean and prepare. Everything happened so fast that it seemed Issa had hardly finished cutting the meat into cooking-size portions when Mariam reappeared from the cookhouse and popped a freshly roasted and beautifully charred kidney into my mouth.

This was the beginning of a day of continuous eating. First, though, Mariam divided about half of the freshly killed meat, still warm from life, into six or eight tidy piles and joyfully directed several of the children hanging about to take them as gifts to other members of the family and, I presume, to neighbors too poor or too friendless to have made a sacrifice of their own. Mariam is by nature a jolly, ebullient person, but I had never before seen her so wholly enraptured. She was like Santa Claus is supposed to be, or an army quartermaster passing out newly delivered rations to a garrison starving under siege. Then we ate and we ate—roast mutton, barbecued mutton, mutton with couscous, mutton with rice and sauce, and then more mutton. Finally, when Mariam was convinced that no one could cope with another bite, she cut the remaining meat into strips and small chunks and put it in the sun to dry. In three or four days everything would be eaten.

What an extravagance Tabaski is in this hard land! If there are half a million families in Mali, nearly half a million sheep are slaughtered on this day alone. And every year for months before the holiday and months afterward, many of these families must go without meat altogether. It would be easy to condemn this, and some do. But I had watched how glad the Keitas were on this day. I had seen their eyes brighten with pride at being able to give to the poor, and even to more affluent relatives, instead of having to accept their own meat as a handout from others. Tabaski is a way of celebrating and sharing the bounty of Allah.

In a very real way, Tabaski is reminiscent of our own American Thanksgiving and of harvest festivals throughout the world. Even as I struggled to put down my final chunk of mutton, I was remembering and reliving those hours magical in memory when my belly ached from its ridiculous load of roast turkey with cranberry sauce, stuffing, mashed potatoes and gravy, candied sweet potatoes, baked squash, creamed onions, hot biscuits, and apple, mince, and pumpkin pies. How the Pilgrims must have stuffed themselves after surviving that first hard and terrifying winter and just before entering the next! To have always just enough is never enough. To feel really safe, it is necessary once in a while to have too much.

"Miss Africa"

Malians, and perhaps most Africans, are completely nonplussed by our American infatuation with privacy. They wonder we don't go mad with loneliness and, if they like us, they worry about us. So I was always getting propositioned, not by the women themselves, but by well-meaning friends and neighbors who were sure they knew someone "just right" for me. Fanta introduced one of her nieces; Kadia brought some possibilities around, so did other friends. And of course there had been a whole series of such episodes in Moribabougou. The woman could cook for me, do my laundry, share my bed, and bring me children. I, as a "wealthy American," could provide her with a secure life. I might even help her emigrate to America. What might we talk about together? In Mali, this question has not much relevance to relationships between men and women.

After I had been settled in for about four months, a friendly interracial couple moved into the house behind me with their two curly-headed blond children and a pretty black nursemaid named Tenin. Only a low wall separated the two houses, and Tenin and I would often wave to one another while I was watering the garden and she was amusing the children or teaching them a few words of Bambara, for even though Cheik, their father, was Malian, their mother was German and the common language of the household was French. One day, Cheik mentioned to me that he thought Tenin was becoming "une peu coquette."

I myself had noticed that she was beginning to fix up a little more and to wear her hair in one of those lovely and complicated Malian coiffeurs, but I hadn't thought of this as especially seductive behavior, at least not with myself as the object. From this time on, though, I found myself watching Tenin more closely, which was easy to do because she was a handsome young woman, tall and well-built, with a wide, ear-to-ear smile accentuated by almost unimaginably white teeth. I privately nicknamed her "Miss Africa."

Soon I found myself paying Tenin small attentions, offering her mangoes from my tree, cold water from my fridge. One day she wore a see-through blouse of some pretty color, I can't remember what, and I shamelessly admired her. The next morning, she walked about for a few hours with no top at all and a sheer, semitransparent skirt.

Of course this display didn't have the same aggressive quality it might have had, say, in Brooklyn, and it may have been, and to some extent surely was, a response to the ninety-five-degree heat we were experiencing that season. Still, it was hard not to suspect that, even in traditionally bare-breasted Africa, women know that men get pleasure from looking at their bodies, especially when those bodies are as beautiful as Tenin's.

A few days after this extraordinary display, Fanta came into my yard and led me by the arm to the wall behind which Tenin was standing, quietly dressed but wearing her wide, shy smile. Fanta wasted no time on preliminaries. "Namory," she said in Bambara, "you are alone here. Tenin can be your wife. Will you accept her?"

I looked at Tenin, sweet and maybe seventeen, standing like merchandise on the other side of the wall, and I searched my feeble Bambara for words of explanation that might gentle my rejection. "No thank you," was the best I could do.

Language Lesson in the Garden

One reason my Bambara was still so weak was that during the summer I had concentrated my language study on French, which I would need in order to communicate with the ENSup administration, and had given Bambara second-class treatment. Once I was settled in, however, I found this weakness in Bambara was impoverishing my relationships with my neighbors: We had our sign and body languages, and these made us want to be friends, but the friendships were hard to consummate. Fanta and I were forever coming to dead ends in our discussions of the garden. Her grandchildren, who had become one of my great delights, came often to visit me in the morning or the evening, and I was reduced to dancing with them or swinging them in the air. I couldn't even talk with El Haji about things that needed doing in the house, because he, too, for all his commercial shrewdness, understood no language but Bambara.

Happily, the Peace Corps had a policy of providing volunteers with continuing language instruction after the formal training period was over. So, beginning in early November, Nèguèdougou Sanogo (nicknamed "Pittsburgh" by many of the volunteers because his first name means "iron city") began stopping by twice a week to tutor me in Bambara. Each lesson was for two hours.

Nèguè, as everyone called him, was for me the perfect teacher, for he was interested in everything. Our classes often drifted after the first hour or so into a kind of bull session—in French, of course, for Nèguè knew little English—on whatever topic either one of us happened to be most interested in at the time. We talked about Islam, about education, about primitive medicine. Nèguè was a voracious reader and shared my interest in black American literature, which he had studied in translation; at one of our meetings, he interrupted a recitation of Victor Hugo to declaim in French and by heart a lengthy poem by Langston Hughes. We talked about my complicated responses to Africa and my occasional loneliness, and he told me of his infant son, in whom he took great pride, and of his reluctance to marry the boy's mother until his education at ENSup was finished.

One particular afternoon when the skies were clear and there was a slight breeze, we held our language lesson out of doors in the shade of the great mango trees in my courtyard. The bare sticks that Fanta had planted were just beginning to leaf out and, after a reasonably disciplined hour or so, Nègue opened a cloth sack he had brought along and took out a small carved figure.

The carving (I have it before me now, well-weathered by sun and rain) was of a naked woman—obviously Senufo from the traditional scarring on the cheeks, and was grotesquely disproportioned. The woman's hands were as big as hams, her legs stumpy, her belly distended. Her full breasts jutted straight forward from her shoulders, and her head with its massive jaw took up a third of the figure's height. Yet, in all that misshapenness there was something marvelously harmonious, even beautiful, and it was clear that the carver had been guided by an idea more compelling to him than the pictorial representation of a woman's body.

It was a fetish, Nègue explained, and it promised rain and a good harvest to the farmer who placed it in his field. "The hands are big for hard work. The oversize head is filled with intelligence. The legs are short to show permanence: She is not going to leave this place. And you can see that she is carrying one child in her womb while still nursing another. A very powerful fetish."

The advance of Islam during the past five hundred years and, to a far lesser extent, the recent incursions of Christianity, largely supplanted the original animism of the West African peoples, and barely 10 percent of Mali's present population still followed the ancient ways. Yet, even among devout Moslems and Christians, there persisted a solid core of belief in the old magic. I asked Nègue, a good Muslim, if he sometimes practiced it.

"It is forbidden," he said and was silent for a long time. Then he added, "Among those farmers who pray to Allah, there are many who feel safer if they also have a fetish in their fields."

In any case, it's evident that all of the really fine carvings here were made by animists as an adjunct to their beliefs, and that the proper question to ask about a work of African art is not, "What is it?" but, "What does it do?"

As usual, one thing led to another and we soon found ourselves talking about the Bahai in Iran, who believe all religions are equally valid efforts to approach the unfathomable mystery of God. Nègue was strongly attracted by their universalist ideals, and there had been news during the week of their persecution by the Shiite followers of the Ayatollah Khomeini in Iran. It seems that, although the Qur'an itself is universalist, and gives nearly equal rank to the teachings of Moses, Jesus, and Mohammed, the latter-day coming of Baha-Ullah, the prophet of the Bahai, was not foretold, and therefore fundamentalist Moslems consider him a false prophet, a phony.

As Nègue talked, I recalled my full-bosomed great-grandmother Emily Olsen, who must surely have been a remarkable woman in her time and place. I was only five or six when she died suddenly, a week before her ninetieth birthday, but I remember vividly her vitality, her fascination with life. Mother Olsen was above all an internationalist, a universalist, and she believed that the absence of a common language was the main barrier to world understanding. She was therefore a great supporter of Esperanto, the artificially constructed "international language" that was supposed to demolish the barriers to communication among peoples, and she traveled the world to attend conferences promoting its use. She organized international pen-pal societies, and once gave me a list of half a dozen children from fascinating places around the world who would like to hear from me if I would learn Esperanto.

What brought her to mind, though, was none of these things, but the fact that she was an ardent Bahai. In fact, there is today in Willamette, Illinois, a Bahai temple so beautiful it is famous throughout the world, and at its entrance is a plaque commemorating great-grandmother's leadership in building the congregation. I've seen this fine temple only in photographs; the real-life memory that clings to my mind is of a great circular basement roofed with tar paper, where the group held its meetings while waiting for the building funds to roll in. Mother Olsen took my brother and me and all my cousins on a tour of it six months before her death.

As he was leaving, Nègue suggested with a smile, "Why don't you leave the fetish in the garden?"

Nèguèdougou was a purist, and he warned that I should not be too friendly with Fanta, as she was a racist. Fanta had been complaining to him that I wasn't paying her enough for my lunches; she had been making the same complaint to me and was afraid I hadn't understood her. When Nègue pointed out that I was already paying her more than the going rate, she became angry. "He is a white man," she told Nègue according to his account, "and you and I are both black. We should stick together."

Nègue was really offended at this and insisted I find another cook, but I had grown too fond of the old woman and refused to believe she was irredeemable.

Mingling with the Diplomats

For Peace Corps volunteers, it's not especially easy to mingle socially with the diplomats, administrators, and others in the expatriate community. Not that these are standoffish. Quite the contrary. Many of them went out of the way to entertain us. But they lived in great houses in the more affluent sections of town; we lived well away in modest apartments in neighborhoods that were more heavily African. They traveled in automobiles; we got about on bicycles, mobylettes, or public transportation. And when we did accept an invitation, we hardly knew how to return it. On my first New Year's Eve in Mali, every American in the country, plus a few non-Americans, was invited to an enormous party at the home of one of the officials of USAID, the Agency for International Development, and a great many of them came.

Apparently the responsibility for hosting these galas is informally rotated from year to year. That year's host, an administrator of middle rank, with thinning red hair and a slight speech defect, occupied a sprawling, beautifully maintained villa, air-conditioned throughout, in one of the "European" quarters of Bamako. The living and dining areas—surely built expressly for parties like this—were huge, white-walled, and tastefully furnished with pseudotropical furniture that would have looked equally chic in Nairobi, Jacarta, Santo Domingo, or Washington, D.C. (I learned later that villas owned or leased by the State Department, wherever they might be, were furnished and decorated on contract by the same American company.)

Most of the party took place outside, however, on the large, screened veranda and under the palm trees in the intricately landscaped garden lighted by torches and electronically protected against mosquitoes. There was taped rock music for dancing indoors and out, and about twenty of the guests who had brought their swimsuits played in the oversized pool.

Pools were a commonplace in the expatriate community here. Almost the only Americans who didn't have grand ones in their yards were the Peace Corps officials, who were expected to live just a bit more humbly than their compatriots and were therefore explicitly forbidden this particular manifestation of luxury. One Assistant Peace Corps Director was reluctantly permitted, for want of an available alternative, to rent a villa with a heart-shaped swimming pool, but she was specifically enjoined from filling the pool with water.

At around five the next afternoon, New Year's Day, Fanta and Aminata and each of Aminata's children came by to wish me Bonne Annee and to receive the traditional gift of 100 francs (about ten cents) apiece. The two older girls, who are about twelve and fourteen, brought New Year's cards with them; one of the cards contained a color photograph of a stunning young Senegalese, daintily posing with her firm breasts bare and a basket of ripe tomatoes on her

41

head. Later, Drissa Traorè, the same young fisherman whose colorful attire had so enchanted me on my first trip to the river in Moribabougou, came by with a brace of freshly caught carp and an embroidered handkerchief neatly folded into a hand-painted card.

A Mysterious Theft

One morning during the holidays, I rose from bed and couldn't find my trousers. Had I, for some inscrutable reason, undressed in the other room? I looked there, but found no trousers. Then I saw that the back door, which I thought I had locked the night before, was wide open. I began to discover other things: The radio was gone from the living room bookcase, the typewriter from the desk, the cassette recorder from the side table in the dining room, and my camera with all its attachments from the dining room cupboard.

Finally, I found my trousers in the courtyard, lying in a heap with all the pockets empty—no wallet, no ID, no credit cards, no U.S. driver's license. And a full month's pay gone as well. The trousers had been taken right out of the bedroom while I slept. I couldn't imagine how a burglar could have tip-toed all through my house, even to the edge of my bed, without waking me. Fanta said he must have used a magic spell.

I reported the matter at the local gendarmerie and a plain-clothes *flic* came over to look around; he wore a short-sleeved work shirt with "Cereal City Window Cleaning Co." lettered on the back and the name "Frank" embroidered over the pocket in front. He was compassionate but not hopeful.

The event was the talk of the neighborhood, and Fanta and her friends and family convened in the yard for hours at a time, commiserating as if I'd lost a dear relative. Even Mariam heard about the theft, way out in Moribagougou, and made a special trip in to bring me small gifts of food and to tell me how sad she was at the news.

5

L'Écôle Normale Supèrieure

About two weeks before the end of September, and shortly after I had moved into Bamako, the faculty of the English Department of ENSup, as L'Ecôle Normale Supèrieure is familiarly called, held its first meeting at the school to assign and schedule classes for the coming year. This was my first opportunity to meet my Malian colleagues and to see the place where I was to begin teaching three weeks hence.

ENSup is beautifully located, overlooking the Niger River and well away from the dust and traffic of downtown Bamako, and it may in its early days have been a congenial place in which to learn. However, cold war diplomacy, official corruption, and military responses to student unrest had destroyed most of its original beauty and utility. Today, now that Mali has achieved a new and hopefully more honest and responsive government, there is talk of rebuilding the school, or at least refurbishing it, but meanwhile time has been taking a further toll.

Beside the wide entrance and securely bolted to the wall still hangs a heroic bronze relief depicting a parade of triumphant youths bearing a giant Soviet flag. An adjacent plaque, now moved to a less conspicuous location, announced that the building had been presented to "the people of Mali by the

43

people of the Soviet Union" in 1968, during the newly independent country's brief experiment with socialism.

Despite its imposing entrance, the interior of the building was a wreck. The ground floor auditorium had a stage but no seats. Classrooms rose in four balconied tiers around a sunken court that might once have been intended as a garden or a pool, but was now simply pavement. The classrooms were walled on two sides with glass, but many of the panes had been broken and others painted over to keep out the heat and glare of the afternoon sun. Each room was filled with the wreckage of desks—metal frames to which wooden shelves and benches had been haphazardly attached. Evidently, two or more students were expected to share each desk, but many desks had no benches, and many benches had no seats. This was the original, or "Russian" wing.

An addition was erected by a grateful American government in 1972 after Lieutenant (later General) Moussa Traorè had seized power and renounced socialism. The two halves were so curiously fitted together that getting from one to the other was a trick in itself. From the entrance, you followed a longish hallway, took a jog-turn right and then left, squeezed through a narrow doorway, and finally stepped up half a foot to another level. It is hard to believe it was by accident that the two structures were so badly fitted together.

Much of the damage to the buildings occurred during a student-faculty strike in 1980 and 1981. Until that time, every student graduating from ENSup and the handful of other institutions of higher learning in Mali was unconditionally guaranteed a lifetime job, if not as a teacher, then in some other branch of the civil service. Eventually, the government became crowded with employees for whom there was neither work nor money and, one day, with the easy abruptness possible in even the mildest of military dictatorships, the promise was broken: Henceforth, education was to be no guarantee of employment.

Since there was and is virtually no private sector in Mali to provide jobs, this seemed to many students an insufferable betrayal of their hopes for escaping the poverty of their villages. A strike, strongly supported by students and teachers at other schools throughout the country, was called, with disastrous results.

Traorè's answer was brutally simple. He arrested the ringleaders, drafted several hundred other students into the army, and closed all of the country's schools for a year. (Recently, after Traorè's violent overthrow, it was learned that at least one of ENSup's student leaders was murdered in prison.) The revolt crushed, the school was reopened the following year and the debris swept out. However, there was no money to make repairs, and the broken doors, desks, and windows remained in place.

The American wing was designed with much less glass than the Soviet, and this might be one of the reasons it was in comparatively better shape.

All students admitted to ENSup must first have graduated from a lycée and passed the baccalaureate examinations, the "*bac.*" This will have given them, presumably, the equivalent of a college education, and at ENSup they study for the *maîtrise* (literally "master's," though everyone told me the two degrees were not at all equivalent). Each student concentrates in a specialized field—English, Russian, chemistry, psychology, etc.—and, after four years of higher education, is licensed as a secondary-school teacher. This is the theory. In actuality, there were and still are virtually no teaching jobs available for any of them.

The most popular field of study at ENSup was English. Many students hoped this would give them a vaguely better shot at finding a job—any kind—with a development organization when they graduated. Some also dreamed (hopelessly, for few visas were available to African students) of emigrating to the U.S. In its four-year curriculum, the English Department had about 350 students.

At the faculty meeting, I was astonished at the number of white faces. Twelve years later, I was the only American, the only native speaker of English, in an English Department of fourteen teachers; then, nine of the fourteen were American Peace Corps volunteers. Surely the students profited by so much exposure to native English speakers, but all of us knew that this gross imbalance owed less to an aspiration to excellence and more to the military government's desire to siphon public funds into private pockets. After all, the Peace Corps teachers were free.

Only three of the department's five Malians were at the meeting—Ousmane Minta, our hyperactive chairman; his friend Mamadou Gueye, who later succeeded him as chairman and was almost as wildly animated as Ousmane; and a soft-spoken assistant professor named Mamadou Doumbia, whose English sounded faintly British because he had taken his master's degree in Yorkshire. The eight-member Peace Corps contingent included, in addition to the six of us newly arrived from Moribabougou, two holdovers from the year before; one of these, a wry-looking fellow named Steve Orvis, was actually beginning his sixth year at ENSup.

A Challenging Course Load

The Malians in the department were mostly interested in teaching the core courses in grammar, linguistics, phonetics, and methodology, and the

45

two Peace Corps veterans had pretty well locked up the courses in British and American literature, so I ended up with second-year "Débat" and two third-year courses, composition and black American literature.

I was told that my composition students would not yet have written anything longer in English than a paragraph and that my responsibility would be to get them ready for the fifty to sixty page graduate theses (called *mémoires*) that they would be required to write in their next and final year. "Débat" was supposed to give students training and experience in argument and public speaking, but how on earth, I asked myself, could I possibly give each of eighty individuals, in two class sections meeting once a week for fifty-five minutes, a chance to speak and be listened to? My third course, in black American literature, which I had never formally studied, quickly became my favorite.

Normally, in an African country I would have expected black American literature to be taught by a black, just as it would almost surely have been taught in the United States. But, while an increasing number of American blacks are enrolling in the Peace Corps today, the only one in Mali at the time was a young woman who had majored in accounting at college and was involved here in the administration of rural credit. For the past two years black American literature had been untaught because no one felt up to teaching it. It was the only literature course available, and I jumped at the opportunity.

When I was going to school in the twenties and thirties, we were taught next to nothing about the history, literature, and lifestyles of the black American people ("Negroes" we called them, always with a capital *N* to deny any lack of respect). Because I liked reading, I became familiar on my own with a few black authors like Langston Hughes, Richard Wright, James Baldwin, Ralph Ellison, and Imamu Baraka (Le Roi Jones as he then called himself). I liked much of what I read, and thought that most mainstream white critics and authors were patronizing of their work.

In the early thirties, while I was finishing up high school in Greenwich, Connecticut, I went one evening to a play in New York and met in the second balcony an aspiring black poet named Owen Dodson. Owen was about my age, on his way in the fall to Bates College, in Maine. We met again three or four times, and at one of these meetings he shared with me an astonishing book called *Cane*, by a black writer of whom I had never heard, Jean Toomer. There was no way I could classify the book as poetry or prose: It was an amalgam of almost every literary form I knew, yet curiously all of a piece.

Owen kept on writing, and much later I found several of his poems in an anthology of black American writers in the school's library. For luck, I decided to include one in the syllabus for my new course.

46

Learning by Doing

In the dozen years since I walked into my first class at L'Ecôle Normale Supèrieure, I have come to look on most of my students as extensions of my growing family. After all, teachers are always parental figures to one degree or another, and at seventy-eight years of age I have more reason than most for such an image. But on that first day in the classroom, the forty politely expressionless black faces confronting me on the other side of my desk seemed less like my children than my adversaries. For, if the truth be told, I scarcely knew what I was doing.

It was during my middle fifties that I came finally to realize that my real vocation was not in advertising, where I had been earning a precarious living, but in teaching, and I was well over sixty before I had accumulated the necessary credentials to make the change. I soon discovered that I had little chance of a finding a conventional full-time job teaching in the U. S., so I volunteered for the Peace Corps, which has no upper age limit. This is how it came to be that I found myself, then sixty-six years old, embarked on a new adventure, teaching French-speaking young Africans to become high-school teachers of English. I was not only inexperienced as a teacher, but I had not had a whit of training in the specialized techniques of teaching English as a foreign language.

My first attempts to call the roll set everyone to laughing. It wasn't just that the names were strange to me; some of them—like Oumar Flathie Toubougazanga Berrè, Blendio Mama Diallo, Ouassa Famba, and Fily Mady Fayèra Sissoko—seemed almost unpronounceable. And, since most of the first names had been taken from the Qur'an, they repeated themselves, so I would have to remember the middle name of every student as well as the first and last. In one class of thirty-six, for example, I had three Mamadous, one Mohammed, one Mamady, and two Mamas (all derivations of the name Mohammed); in another, I had five Moussas (Moses), three with the same last name. Worse, there are in each ethnic group in Mali only a limited number of family names, handed down proudly for at least five centuries—the local equivalents of Cabot, Lodge, Smith, Cohen, and Levy. In the second section of my class in black American literature, which took in surnames beginning with the letters S through Y, there were three Sidibes, two Tambouras, two Toures, and thirteen Traorès!

Happily, most of the women had musical, easy-to-remember names like Mariètou, Habibatou, Adizatou, Kadiatou, and Marie Yvonne, but, alas, women accounted for less than 10 percent of the enrollment.

Whatever their names, my students' English was almost impossible for me to understand. It wasn't spoken with a French accent, even though this was

47

officially a French-speaking country and French was the language of instruction in the elementary schools and lycées. It was something distinctly Malian, or perhaps West African. "Cat" sounded like "cot" (though the *t* might sometimes come out like a *d*), "good" rhymed with "food," and the vowels in words like "bite," "bit," and "beat" were virtually indistinguishable. In multisyllabic words, the stress might fall anywhere at all.

As a warm-up for exercises in public speaking, I asked pairs of students in my second-year Débate class to interview one another for a couple of minutes and then to make two-minute "platform" introductions to their classmates. They took gaily to the idea and presented their partners with great enthusiasm and occasionally, I think, with eloquence, but I knew as little about my students afterwards as before.

The problem of understanding was not one-sided. No matter how slowly, how deliberately I spoke, at least half the students in the room would stare at me in blank incomprehension. Yet they seemed to understand each other's English, and in all of my classes a handful of the brightest could be counted on to serve as interpreters between the majority and myself. They didn't translate, of course, for the use of any language but English was forbidden; they simply restated in their own West African accents what I had been struggling hopelessly to make clear in my standard American one. I began to rethink the speed with which my classes could progress.

I should not have worried about my students' willingness to accept me as their teacher. Despite the lack of books and the dirty and crowded classrooms, despite the emptiness of the pot at the end of the rainbow, most students tried hard and kept trying, and my own inexperience, which had so worried me at first, was completely overlooked. In fact, because I was older than all the other professors at school, I was held to be wiser as well.

Predictably, my favorite course turned out to be black American literature. It was actually a course in black American history and civilization, with literature embedded, because my Malian students had no understanding of how blacks live and have lived in America, and thus of the context from which their poetry, fiction, and drama spring. I'm sure from the enthusiasm with which they worked that it was one of their favorite courses, too.

The English Club Puts on a Show

At the beginning of the term, I had helped organize an English Club to give the more ambitious students a forum in which they could use their English outside the classroom. Leaders of the club persuaded individual Americans from organizations like the Embassy and the Agency for International Development

48

to lead panel discussions on subjects like "Religion in America" and "American Styles of Courtship and Marriage." One of the club's early programs was a dramatic reading by students of "Poets of the Black American Renaissance." An aspiring dramatist named Boubacar Beico Diallo directed the production and students wrote their own commentaries on the poems. I coached the readers on their pronunciation and on the interpretation of the poems.

We rehearsed the presentation in my courtyard, and each evening for a week I watched a dozen eager young Africans struggle with varying success to master the language, rhythms, and ideas of poems written by American blacks during the 1920s and 1930s, which is as far as my literature course had managed to get them thus far. I vividly remember listening to the youngest of our performers, Tamba Keita, a shy and serious first-year student from a small Malinkè village to the west, with a voice like Ezio Pinza's, grapple with Langston Hughes' loving description of Harlem as "a chocolate custard pie of a town" when he himself had never heard of Harlem nor seen or tasted a chocolate custard pie. I listened to Boubacar Belco as he asked for Countée Cullen:

> What is Africa to me:
> One three centuries removed
> From the scenes his fathers loved?
> coming at last to the confession that, despite his
> Christian veneer,
>
> Lord, I fashion dark gods, too,
> Daring to give even you
> Dark despairing features.

When, after a week of nightly rehearsals, the students presented the program at the Cultural Center of the American Embassy, it was a smashing success. As a finale, Boubacar had turned excerpts from Langston Hughes' "Montage of a Dream Deferred" into a finger-snapping, foot-stomping production number culminating in an impassioned choral reading of the poem beginning, "What happens to a dream deferred? / Does it dry up / like a raisin in the sun?" and ending, "Or does it explode?"

The cheering, clapping, and whistling went on so long afterwards that the cast was obliged to repeat the entire forty-minute performance from beginning to end.

"Débat" was another story.

I had started the year with the stereotyped notion that my job was to teach the subject, that is, how to speak in public. But it didn't take me more

49

than a day to realize that the sheer number of students—eighty divided into two sections of forty each—and the fact that I met with each section for only one hour a week—made speaking at length a practical impossibility for everyone. I gave them short exercises in enunciation, in gesture, in the expression of feeling and conviction, and spent several class periods discussing logic and "techniques of argumentation." And for a total of six minutes per week, individual students delivered brief oral reports (necessarily limited to three sentences each!) on aspects of Malian culture.

The students had fun waving their arms and crying to the heavens, and I picked up some fragmentary cultural information about the ceremony of teamaking, but I was sure no one was learning anything worthwhile. In near despair, I chucked the role of instructor and became instead an organizer: The students would have to learn from themselves and from each other. (I've learned since that this is a standard technique in teaching large classes, but I thought at the time that I had invented it.)

First, I split each section into two groups, with roughly twenty students in each, and hunted up a vacant classroom so the groups could meet separately. The two groups then selected their own leaders and the topics they wanted to discuss—abortion, the prohibition of alcohol, Islam as a state religion, prostitution, women's liberation, and so on.

Lance Mathieson, husband of a fellow Peace Corps teacher and a former intercollegiate debater, came to class one day and explained how debates are organized, with one team taking the affirmative side of a proposition and the other the negative, and then the two teams changing places and supporting the opposite view. I assigned teams and topics and supervised one practice debate and a straw vote to determine the winners.

My wearisome role was now superficial. I merely moved back and forth between classrooms, listening when I could but mostly lending the moral force of my interest. At first, students tended to load their arguments in favor of the side of the proposition they personally favored. Soon, though, they discovered that the real challenge, the real fun was to win, not just one side of the debate, but both. Preparation became more intense, teamwork more evident, and the impromptu discussions and peer-critiques that followed each session became so enthusiastic that classes sometimes continued well into the recess periods.

Habibatou Debates the Practice of Excision

One of the topics selected by the students was the practice of excision, or female circumcision, a difficult subject for most students to debate in public, though all held decided views. It seemed to me that they did astonishingly well, and one student in particular made two presentations I will not easily forget.

Habibatou Niaré was the beauty of Section IIB. She was dark and full-featured, with large eyes, wide, flaring nostrils, and a high forehead, which she accentuated by drawing her hair back into an intricate knot on the top of her head—a real Bambara beauty. The most notable aspect of Habibatou's appearance, though, was her carriage. I have often used the word "queenly" to describe the rooted way all Malian women, habituated from childhood to carrying heavy loads on their heads, walk and stand. Habibatou's carriage was more than queenly; it was imperial. She was tall and large-boned, and when she turned to speak to someone she didn't merely turn her head, but swiveled her entire upper torso, like a dancer. I would have thought her topic an especially difficult one for a young woman in a class predominantly male, but she carried it off with no apparent qualm, speaking with equal vigor—and for the full five minutes allowed—on each side of the question.

I especially liked the way "Habi" handled the negative side, avoiding the commonplace and phony clichés that excision somehow minimizes adultery and prevents prostitution, and instead went straight to the sad core of the rite—the initiation of young African girls into the hard life of womanhood.

Each student was required to submit a written outline of his and her oral presentations. Here, unedited, are Habibatou's:

AFFIRMATIVE
Resolved that excision should be prohibited by law.

Dear friends, before doing any other thing, I should make you know what does excision mean. Excision, you know, is an act of removal. In this precise case, it is the cutting out of the clitoris which is the erectile organ of the vulva. So knowing that, do you think it is necessary to excise? I think no.

First, everybody knows that every part in a human body has a precise role to perform. So dear friends, we should not make any change in this natural organization of our bodies.

Second, you know that the vulva is the most important and precious organ in a woman's body because it is the first sign of femininity and also because of the functions it performs. In this organ the clitoris is the most important element for it helps women in their sentimental activities and also in their maternity, precisely when they are delivering. When the clitoris is erected, the vulva expands, the mother is excited, and things go easily. But if the mother is excised, complications like the rent of the organ or the fatigue of the mother may happen and lead to death.

Third, excision can make a woman frigid. You all know what is frigidity. So we should avoid that, because in a family both partners should get a maximum of satisfaction in their common sentimental activities which support the household. Frigidity can be cause of divorce.

Fourth, you know excision requires a lot of care. We can easily lose our lives in this operation. Tetanus and excessive bleeding have been the most frequent complications of excision and have destroyed many lives.

So because of these facts, let's prohibit excision to preserve our health.

NEGATIVE

Excision should not be prohibited. Why?

You know that every country has its own culture, its own civilization. So why do you want us to prohibit an element of ours? To prohibit excision is to turn against our tradition and also against our religion. You know Islam is our main religion, and you know that it is religion which brought excision to our country. According to Muslim people, a woman who is not excised is unclean.

Second, as you must know, excision is one of our ways to integrate the society. You know that to get to the state of a woman, a girl has to be excised. Then she gets married and is considered as a complete woman capable of facing life.

Third, excision is part of our education. You know, when girls are excised, they are gathered in an older woman's house for cure. This old woman, in addition to the cure, performs the role of supervisor and advisor. In short, she has the task of a teacher. She teaches good attitudes, good habits, obedience, sociability.

Fourth, everybody knows that the clitoris is the most sensitive point in a woman's body. So any cruel act at this level is hard to support. This is to say, excision is the first experience in a woman's life which prepares her to endure. It is also a way to reduce the sensitivity of a woman so that she can prevent herself from flirting for a long time.

These are some reasons why we should not prohibit excision.

I Am Approached by an Intermediary

I had now been in Mali almost a year, and the continued exhortations of friends and colleagues, as well as the inviting glances I kept receiving from young Malian women, were beginning to persuade me that perhaps it was indeed true that in this culture age need be no barrier to romance. I had been mulling this interesting possibility for several months when, one morning during a break between classes, Mamadou Doumbia, a male student in one of my third-year sections, approached me just as composition class was about to begin.

"Have you noticed what Adizatou is wearing today?" he asked.

Adizatou was a dainty young woman of the type the French call *mignonne*. She was one of my brightest students, though so shy I had become aware of her only through the quality of her written work. This day, however, she was hard not to notice, for she was dressed to kill, if that's the way to describe her appearance, in a really splashy French-African robe of many colors, with a dozen ribbons and bows stitched on for good measure.

"She is wearing it especially for you," said Mamadou.

My bachelordom let me in for a lot of kidding from students as well as from neighbors, so I passed off the question with a smile and a compliment. Mamadou was insistent. "See, she has brought her twin sister here so you can choose between them." And there beside Adizatou was another handsome young woman, even tinier. "Which do you prefer? You must choose one."

I was still not catching on, but I felt I should tell him I liked Adizatou better, as she was my student.

"Good," said Mamadou. "I am her intermediary. When would you like to see her?"

By this time, it was evident to me that this was not a joke but an earnest example of the way things are often done here in Mali, and that he was genuinely acting on Adizatou's behalf and with her knowledge. Because of Adizatou's shyness, I had no clear perception of her as a person, but she was bright and lovely so I decided to give the adventure a shot.

"Would she like a dish of ice cream some day after class?" (If I had been in Mali longer, I would have known that the appropriate site for the rendezvous would have been my house, not a restaurant.)

"Yes," responded Mamadou with a toothy smile. "She would like that very much. Which day will be better for you—Monday or Tuesday?" He was as well-focused as an insurance salesman from Prudential.

"Monday, at six o'clock," I said.

We met as a threesome in a small French *patisserie* in the center of town. A lovely, soft-spoken, almost silent-spoken girl—mostly yes or no answers to my questions, with unhelpful interpolations now and then from our intermediary. Probably dynamite under that composed exterior, but what a labor it would be to find out!

Still, I had absorbed an important cultural lesson and learned as well that not all the flirtatious approaches made to me during the past year had been intended as jokes. I made up my mind to give the matter another try, for it had been a long time since I had enjoyed the companionship of a woman, even one manifestly too young. This time, though, I would make my own selection, someone bolder, more assertive. Habibatou came first to mind, but I knew she was engaged, so I turned my thoughts toward one of the more vivacious students in my debate class, not as statuesque as Habibatou but just as lovely. I will call her Aisha.

6

Aisha

N èguèdougou was ecstatic when I invited him to be my intermediary, and on the very next day he dropped by to tell me that Aisha would come to the house the following Sunday afternoon. He would personally fetch her.

I may have suggested that Aisha was beautiful. Actually, she was not, just great fun to look at. Her nose, viewed from three-quarter profile, seemed to turn up neatly at the tip—what we used to call a "ski-jump" nose. *Retroussé.* Broad nostrils, a chin that receded just a little and so helped to give her rather small mouth a pursed look, as if someone had told her to "pucker up" or, more accurately, as if she had puckered up without being told. Her eyes were large, brown of course, and her black lashes were long and curly, the kind many American women buy and paste on.

Aisha paid a lot of attention to her clothes. At school she wore traditional African *boubous*—rich, flowing robes made of yards of brilliantly colored cotton—with coordinating headbands that came almost to her eyebrows, and shoes and jewelry to match. It was hard to get much of an impression of her figure under all that fabric but, like all the women in Mali, accustomed since childhood to carrying everything from school-books to huge bundles of laundry balanced on their heads, Aisha stood and moved like part of the earth.

I knew that some—I hoped not all—of Aisha's motivation for coming over was to practice her English. She was a diligent B student, liked school, and worked hard in all her classes. Since our first "date" was to be in company of our intermediary Nèguèdougou, who spoke elegant French but was more than uncertain in English, I was concerned about how to handle the language situation. I needn't have been. After about ten minutes of French, and just as I was thinking, "Oh, how disappointed she must be!" Aisha turned to Nèguè, who is not only male but at least ten years older, and said—an almost undreamed-of act of assertion by a Malian woman— "Nèguèdougou, you'll just have to learn English!" And that put an end to French for the day.

This did not, however, make the conversation easy, and often I felt I was following a nonexistent trail in the moonless dark. "How do you like school?" "What is your favorite subject?" "Why do you want to be an English teacher?" "What does your father do?" "Does he have several wives?" ("No, just my mother.") "What village do you come from?" ("We have always lived in Bamako.") All the questions from me, none from Aisha. And yet we seemed to feel increasingly comfortable with one another. She told me I was "very coura- geous" to have "such a big house" for myself. She was sure I was a "very good cook." "Very" was almost her favorite word, and she pronounced it with enthusiasm. I told her she was very beautiful.

Since Aisha was coming over in midafternoon, I had told Nèguè I would prepare a nice fruit salad of oranges, pineapple, and bananas, with some iced tea and cookies. He was aghast.

"What, no meat?" I pointed out that four o'clock was hardly dinner time. "It doesn't matter," he lectured. "In Mali, people always like to eat meat, and if you invite a woman to your house she will expect to eat meat, no matter what the time." Since it was then too late to buy and cook fresh meat, I rushed out to a neighboring rotisserie and bought what turned out to be the toughest, most overcooked slabs of mutton I had ever tasted. They were a sensational success.

Aisha insisted on washing the dishes in her magnificent clothes, and I told her I liked that. Finally she said, "I want to go." We had a brief tutorial inter- lude in which I explained that Americans never say they "want" to go, even if true, but always, "Really, I must go." I walked her to the bashée stop, with Nèguè trailing discreetly behind.

A small difficulty: Nèguè, who had watched our farewell from a distance, exclaimed incredulously afterwards, "But you didn't give her any money for the bashée! You should have given her five hundred or even a thousand francs."

"But Nègue, the *bashée* costs only eighty francs [about eight cents at the current exchange rate]!"

"Never mind. You're not in America now. You should have given her five hundred francs. And you must give her a thousand when she comes back next week."

Two weeks later, Aisha returned. This time, no Nègue. Head-to-head confrontation. *Tête-à-tête.* The meat was ready—*carbonnade flammande*, a light beef stew cooked in beer and fennel. (I didn't mention the beer to Aisha, though the alcohol had been thoroughly cooked out of it.) She suggested we eat outside in the garden and, while I was getting the food from the kitchen, Aisha carried out a pair of bamboo armchairs from the house. Then she looked astonished at the two separate plates I had set on the table and exclaimed,

"But we must eat *together!*"

So back to the kitchen went the plates and the forks and the spoons. I put everything into a single bowl and we ate Malian style, with our right hands. When eating this way before, I'd paid most of my attention to the strange business of using my hands as utensils; now I understood that it was the common bowl—the *sharing* of the meal—that was important.

Aisha was a gracious young lady, with a lot of class, and I'm sure her Malian table manners were exquisite. Still, it is hard to eat stew with one's fingers.

Like so many vitamin-conscious people nowadays, I cook and eat my potatoes with their jackets on. Aisha gracefully peeled each one, licked the gravy from her fingers, and then delicately flicked the peelings onto the paving stones for the nonexistent goats and chickens to eat or for Fanta to sweep up in the morning. Within hours they were desiccated.

Aisha was an enthusiastic person. First, there was this business of "very." But all her speech was packed with intensifiers, exclamations, and underlines. "Professor *Orvis?* Oh, *yes!* He's *such* a good teacher!" "Oh, yes! I love *all* my teachers! They really know their *matter!*" "African lit? Oh, I *love* African lit! I love *all* my courses!" This might have sounded gushy on the lips of an American debutante, but in Aisha's lilting, French-African accent, this enthusiasm was as life-giving as the fountain Ponce de Leon never found.

I told Aisha of Nègue's comment on the *bashée* money. "I didn't forget," I told her. "It just didn't occur to me because, in America, we don't usually give girls money for transportation unless we are riding together. But I do want to learn Malian ways. I don't expect to become African, any more than I expect you to become American, but it will be good to learn each other's ways."

"Oh, yes! That will be *very* good!" Aisha exclaimed.

And that was our day. Aisha said, "Really, I *must* go," and together we walked to the *bachée* stop. Remembering our first visit, I held out 1,000 francs.

56

She laughed and opened her hand. She had her own 80 francs all ready for the driver.

Two weeks later on a wearying Saturday afternoon—stifling heat, consultation with a near-hopeless student about his dissertation on the poetry of Whitman, four hours of stencil-typing for my class in black American lit, last-minute shopping for a solitary dinner (no convenience foods here). Unwashed. Wearing my most ragged clothes. Watering the garden. And then miraculously, like the mango tree, which bears its succulent fruit during the driest, most inhospitable season of the year, Aisha appeared at my gate, dressed as if for a wedding. She wanted my comments on a short dialogue she had written for her class in the methodology of teaching.

She'd done a fair job, but I suggested that the ending—the punch line—was a little flat. She fixed it while I biked out for fresh bread and brought butter and a jug of cold water from the kitchen. In fifteen minutes she was ready to leave, for she was one of a group of four students who had agreed to study for the final exam together, and she was already overdue. I walked with her to the *bashée*. Moslems are great spitters; they learn this during the fast of Ramadan when, for thirty days, they are forbidden to swallow even their own saliva between sunrise and sunset, Aisha spat into the dust at least half a dozen times on our short walk.

"I could see last week that you obey me very well," she said.

"Obey?"

"I mean, you respect me very much."

A brief review of idiomatic English: She knew I was beginning to like her a lot. "That's true," I said as the *bashée* arrived on cue and took her away, clutching her eighty-franc fare.

Immersed as I was in an almost totally black society, I often wondered how anyone as richly colored as Aisha could care for anyone as pallid as myself. One Saturday afternoon, while we were sitting side by side on the bamboo settee, she held her bare forearm next to mine and announced,

"I *love* the color of your skin!"

I was astonished. "You do? You really do? But Aisha, it is *your* skin that is beautiful!"

Aisha had a special smile—lips pressed tightly together, mouth stretched from ear to ear—that she saved for moments when she was especially pleased with herself. She threw me one of these now. "Then we are both satisfied," she said.

On her next visit, I asked about her parents. Would they approve of her seeing an American man?

"My father is an educated man," said Aisha. "He works in the post office. He has promised me that when I finish school I can choose any man I want. But until then, I will do no bad thing."

I knew what Aisha meant by "no bad thing," but she was just about to finish her sophomore year and graduation was a good two years away. This kind of wait was not what I had in mind when I asked Nègue to bring her over for our first date. "Aisha, look at my white hairs. It isn't sensible for me to wait two years for anything."

"If you know my mind, you will wait two years." She explained that when she first entered ENSup her father had made her promise solemnly, with her mother and older sisters as witnesses, that she would not marry or even speak to a man until she had earned her degree. In return, he gave her his promise that, contrary to the family's tribal customs (they were Fula, proud descendents of a seminomadic cattle-herding people), he would not choose a husband for her. "When I finish school, I can choose any man I want. Anyone."

"Even me?"

"Of course you."

"And your mother, will she agree?"

"Never worry about my mother. Women are nothing in this country."

What a delicious agony! Leaving aside Aisha's extraordinary personal advantages, I found it thrilling, so close to my sixty-seventh birthday, even to consider waiting two years for any kind of good at all. It would be like taking immortality for granted.

A Visit to the Marabout

Despite the increasing heat, the air was still dry and, in late afternoon when the sun was low in the sky, it was quite comfortable out-of-doors, so Nègue and I got into the habit of taking long walks during our Bambara lessons. Our favorite walk took us past the Soviet embassy half a dozen blocks to the south, with its impressive apartment complex where the embassy's employees were obliged to live, and across fields and irrigated gardens that reached all the way to the river. There were bits of construction here and there to indicate that Bamako was expanding at a rapid, perhaps a too rapid, rate, but the scene was predominantly rural. Here and there the river had spread out haphazardly over the flat land, littering it with tiny ponds and imperceptibly moving streams. At a few crossings, small boys waited with their pirogues to ferry farmers and townspeople across.

On one such afternoon, Nègue had taken me to the bank of one of these streams to see fifteen or twenty bare-breasted young women standing knee-deep in the water, washing clothes. "Don't let them catch you staring," he had

58

cautioned. "They will think you are very rude." One shapely, half-clothed laundress stood up at full length and waved to me, and I waved back.

On another walk, Nègue—who seemed to know everyone of interest—introduced me to an elderly man who, he said, had retired a few years ago from an important position in the government. With the money he had accumulated—Nègue did not say how—he was able to buy several dozen hectares of rich bottom land and to plant it with bananas, pineapple, and mangoes. According to Nègue, he was one of the richest men in Bamako. We sat on steel-and-plastic lawn chairs, talked about the criminal depredations of President Moussa Traorè, and watched the river water surge rhythmically from the end of a hose that must have been six inches in diameter.

This time, Nègue was taking me to meet his friend Mama, the *marabout*. A *marabout* is a seer, a traditional Islamic wise man who can foretell the future and sometimes improve it a little with the aid of potions and spells. Mama was a chunky, bald, and very jolly man of about forty-five, and a Boso who, like all members of that ethnic group, takes his livelihood from the river. We found him at the river's edge with a small boy I took to be his son, shaping mud and straw into bricks. Obviously delighted at the prospect of exchanging his menial chore for something more interesting, and possibly even lucrative, Mama greeted us with enthusiasm and quickly washed the mud from his arms and legs. Then he led us into a small mud-brick house with an arched roof of reeds, ceiled on the inside with printed fabric and furnished with an oversized cotton mattress and several disorderly heaps of old books and ledgers.

The three of us sat lotuslike on the mattress and, from behind one of the piles of books. Mama produced a small cotton bag of cowries, those tiny, vaginal-shaped shells that a hundred years ago served here as money. He took out a handful and, after a moment's meditation, cast them lightly on the center of the mattress, much as if preparing to read the I-Ching. Apparently the pattern in which the cowries fell was meaningful, for after a few moments he took up a battered ledger and thumbed to a page handwritten in Arabic. Then he addressed me in Bambara, for Mama, though an Arabic scholar, knew no French. Nègue translated.

The project I had in mind, said Mama (neither Nègue nor I had thus far revealed my "project" to him), was hazardous, but success was nevertheless certain if I would follow his advice. Then, step by step, in the way of fortune-tellers everywhere, he managed to establish that my question concerned a woman.

"It is clear that she returns your feelings strongly," Nègue translated, "but her parents will cause a problem. You must keep your feelings secret from them until you have possessed her entirely. Then she will be able to oppose them."

59

To fortify my chances, Mama urged me to make a "sacrifice." I must buy and cook a small fish and eat it in solitude, without rice or other accompaniment, meanwhile contemplating a vision of my secret wish.

That evening I ate the fish, and during the night I had two dreams.

In the first, Aisha and I were walking through Grand Central Station, and I was struggling under the weight of our heavy bags. She became impatient, snatched them from me, piled them on top of her head, and marched grandly out to the train.

In the second, we were having dinner with my sister Nancy in Nancy's Boston apartment. Aisha gracefully flicked her potato peels onto the Karastan carpet.

Promises and premonitions!

A Change of Seasons

In semitropical countries like Mali, the year does not divide itself, as it does in our temperate zone, into the four seasons of spring, summer, fall and winter. Instead, the Malian year consists of just two grossly unequal seasons—a long dry season and a relatively short rainy one. In the dry season, which begins typically in mid-September, the climate is dominated by the thirsty Harmattan winds sweeping down from the Sahara. For eight and sometimes nine months or more, west-central Mali receives scarcely a drop of a rain, its ponds and streams are sucked dry, and the air itself turns red with dust. Then in late April or mid-May, just when it seems that every herb, tree, and living creature must soon perish from drought, there is a gracious shift in the currents of wind, and moisture-laden air from the Indian Ocean flows westward to drive the bone-dry desert air out to sea. The last six weeks of the dry season, when the air is saturated with moisture but the rain refuses to fall, are rightly called the "hot season."

"Wait until April," my students had told me. "You won't be happy teaching afternoon classes then."

And now the hot season had actually arrived. For weeks the temperature crept toward the 100 mark by half a degree a day, and now, a week before the beginning of May, it was consistently over 105 and still rising. Worse, the air was so dense with humidity that my skin was continually wet, and yet still the rain refused to fall. I showered three to four times a day and washed my hands as compulsively as Lady Macbeth, but still the salts accumulated on my chest, in the crooks of my elbows, and on the backs of my hands. Even to breathe was laborious.

It was my hands especially that troubled me. The problem began with small, puffy, red blotches on my knuckles and on the outside of my thumbs. I

60

took these to be some kind of heat rash until they spread to cover the backs of my hands entirely; these became so sensitive that the skin would break open at the slightest friction—when I washed, for example, or when I reached into my pockets for change.

"Are you sure they don't itch?" asked Rebecca, our pretty medical officer. No, I advised her.

"Maybe it's psoriasis," she suggested helpfully. "It comes with getting old, and there isn't much you can do about it except to control it a little with steroids." She gave me some ointment.

At school, everyone asked about my hands. Even Aisha, "It's just the sun," I told them.

The hot season is especially debilitating to Moslems when it coincides with the fast of Ramadan, as it did my first year in Mali. During the fast, which lasts for thirty days, no Muslim may allow a bite of food or a drop of water to pass down his throat between the hours of sunrise and sunset. Even to swallow one's own saliva is forbidden. In the afternoon, government workers, awake since the predawn morning meal and without food or water since, dozed at their desks. Officials of international aid organizations whose employees were better motivated and better supervised, complained nonetheless that half of each afternoon was wasted. Many students, too, were weak with fasting, and classes were dull and listless.

One afternoon, as I was biking home through the city, the sky darkened suddenly. Streaks of lightning crisscrossed overhead, thunder cracked, and frightening, gale-force winds sent leaves, branches, rubbish, and occasional items of merchandise hurtling dangerously through the streets. I dove, bicycle and all, into the nearest doorway where a baker's dozen of Malian men and women had already invited themselves for shelter.

Moments later, the rain itself arrived, not falling in any conventional way at all, but flying horizontally through the cluttered air, like tracer bullets from a hydraulic machine gun up the street. There was no escape from the torrent, and I was deeply thankful for the open vestibules that are characteristic of most Malian houses in the city.

While we waited together for a gap in the storm, a young man emerged from inside the house, bearing a tray with four shot glasses of strong, sweet Malian tea. He handed one to me and to each of the three refugees nearest. I knew my Malian manners and, after one cautious sip, gulped down the hot, sticky stuff in a swallow, so my glass could be washed and refilled for the next.

The downpour continued for at least an hour and drenched Bamako, I learned later, with more than an inch of water.

Final Exams

With the end of the dry season came also the end of classes and the beginning of the distasteful job of examining and grading students. As in most European schools, the program at ENSup is fueled by exams: Students are expected to work, not to gain knowledge, but to pass their final exams; professors are obliged to teach so their students can pass them. Writing the exams was especially tedious, because three separate versions had to be readied for every course: one primary version for the *session ordinaire;* one *examen de sécurité* in case the first was leaked or stolen; and finally an *examen de rattrapage,* a second-chance exam for students who failed the first time around.

When the fateful week of the *session ordinaire* arrived, teachers were assigned, in pairs, to monitor the various examining rooms. Then, at each day's end, the teachers would pick up the completed exams for their own students and take them home. By the end of the week, I had accumulated 165 essay exams, with three days to grade them.

During a lull in the schedule, Bob Kliessen, a fellow volunteer whose father ran a fish farm in Kansas, was bewailing his misfortune in having to fail one of the prettiest girls in the school because "she simply can't understand an English sentence."

Souleyman Ba, a tall and spectre-thin Malian colleague, was incredulous. "How can you fail a pretty girl? Do what I do. At the beginning of the term, put your classes through a short quiz and give failing grades— terrible grades, fours and fives—to the best-looking girls. When one of them complains, invite her to your house for special help. Believe me," said Souleyman, twisting his skinny lips into what he must have supposed to be a smile, "if the girl has a brain in her head, neither one of you will fail the test." All the Malians on the faculty were ashamed of Souleyman, but they were afraid to say or do anything because it was widely believed he had "connections."

Judging the model lessons and *memoires* of the fourth-year students was more interesting. As one member of a jury of three, I visited the lycées where they had been practice-teaching all year and evaluated their anxious performances in the classroom. After these model lessons came the *memoires,* and I sat on another jury while a dozen students, one at a time, presented and defended the dissertations on which they had been working all year. Happily, all my students passed, though poor Bakary's long essay on the history of jazz barely got by. Reaching for a top grade, he brought some tapes to the jury room to illustrate his presentation but, in his nervousness, he got them hopelessly mixed up and retired in confusion; only his written work saved him from failure.

At last came the electric morning toward which the entire school year had been pointing. Loudspeakers were set up in the auditorium and on the balconies outside, and school desks with their attached benches were dragged out of the classrooms to provide seating. Around eight o'clock, nearly two hours before the scheduled ceremony, ENSup's eight hundred to nine hundred students began streaming into the building with their families and friends and squeezing into the small auditorium and the courtyard outside, or settling themselves on benches and desktops on one of the three balconied floors surrounding. Some draped themselves precariously on the railings.

Nothing was ready but no one seemed to mind. Finally, after a wait of at least three hours, an excited buzz rippled over the crowd, and I could see signs of movement in the densely packed area around the stairs. The sleepy-eyed Director General of the school worked his way to a microphone on the second-floor balcony, supported by a contingent of administrators in their best traditional dress, and, in his characteristically inaudible voice, introduced a dignitary from the Ministry of Education. I never caught the functionary's name, but it made no difference, for he gave no speech of congratulations or encouragement, but simply began reading, department by department, class by class, the names of those who had passed the year.

This public reading was the students' first chance to know officially whether they had passed or failed, for their grades on the final exams, even the scores of seniors on *mémoires* and model lessons, had been kept strictly secret. There was much delighted hand shaking and back slapping among the successful students, but it was an agonizing time for those on the borderline, and a humiliating one for those whose names were not read out, for neither they nor their classmates had been certain of their failure until this public moment. During the reading, several students held my hand for support and, when she did not hear her name announced, Kadiatou Maiga, a tall and graceful young woman from the desert country near Timbuktoo, hurled herself sobbing into my arms.

Nèguèdougou was one of the successful ones; he graduated from the Department of Psychology and Pedagogy first in his class, with a grade average the equivalent of an American A. Aisha also passed the year and now had only two years to wait before she could choose a man for herself.

Late in the afternoon, Aisha showed up at the house to receive my congratulations. She had obviously prepped for the occasion, for she leaped into the conversation without preamble.

"Ask me some questions about New Jersey."

Taken aback by this unexpected demand, I was about to oblige when she went on speaking, if no question had been necessary.

"The capital of New Jersey is Trenton. George Washington won a famous battle there during the American Revolution. Who is the mayor of Trenton?"

I allowed that I didn't know, but told her that one of New Jersey's senators had been a famous basketball player named Bill Bradley.

"*William* Bradley," she corrected triumphantly, and pulled out a school notebook with the letters *U.S.A.* elegantly hand-lettered on the cover. "Senator *William* Bradley! Athletes make *wonderful* politicians. You can *trust* athletes!"

She opened her notebook to a page headed New Jersey. "See! I have been reading about New Jersey. I *like* New Jersey!"

She had certainly been making a small study of it. There in her notebook, neatly lettered in the small, legible hand she had learned in primary school, was a page of fascinating facts about the state of my official residence: its area, its population, its principal cities and industries, and much more.

"Do you know I am an athlete? I was the best girl in my lycée for climbing the rope. I mean the fastest."

I looked closely at her trim little figure, almost entirely disguised by her loosely hanging robe. She didn't look like a rope-climber.

"Here, feel my shoulder. Feel how strong it is."

I felt. This was my first opportunity to touch any part of Aisha's body other than her hands, and she was right. It was a very solid, well-constructed shoulder. "Let me feel the other one, too," I asked. She seemed not to mind, so I massaged both shoulders gently. "Very strong," I said.

At this point, I remembered that Nèguèdougou had said, "If you want to win a Malian girl, you must embrace her." Mama the *marabout* had given me similar advice. Aisha herself seemed relaxed and welcoming under my slow massage, and so, confident of the moment, I drew her gently toward me.

Immovable object! Iron-willed resistance! I tried once more to test if my apprehensions were misleading me. They were not.

"I'm sorry," said Aisha. "It is my fault. I made a mistake."

A mistake? To refuse me? No, not that. To lead me on? But really she hadn't meant to. She just didn't want to be kissed and was groping for a way to say no without actually saying it, for that would shame me. Did she feel I had insulted her?

"Oh, *no!*" she exclaimed. "When you want to kiss me, that tells me you like me *very* much."

Well, so much for Nèguèdougou's advice. When I chided him later, he stopped short of saying he didn't believe her. "There may still be a few such girls in Bamako, from very strict traditional families, but times are changing fast. I doubt if you can find another girl like that in all of ENSup."

64

Remembering the enthusiasm with which Aisha's female classmates had debated the topic of abortion earlier in the year, so did I. I repeated to Nèguè what Aisha had told me at one of our first meetings, that she had to be home each night before dark and that she had never in her life been to a movie theater or to a restaurant.

To which he replied noncommittally, "You have chosen for yourself a very old-fashioned girl."

Balamine's Field

Despite my deepening relationship with Fanta and her grandchildren, I kept my attachment to my original family in Moribabougou. Religiously, one Sunday a month, I pedaled out to the village and once in a while either Birama or Mariam would come into the city to see me, always bringing with them a small gift of fruit. Once they brought me a fresh fish, caught that morning by their neighbor Drissa Traorè. One Saturday afternoon, Aisha proposed that we take a *bashée* and visit Moribabougou together.

On the half-hour ride out, I noticed that Aisha sat well apart from me and conversed only with the other women passengers. Once arrived in the village, however, she apparently decided that the risk of exposure was minimal, and she marched boldly beside me, carrying the sack of cola nuts and other small gifts we had selected for the family.

This was the first open acknowledgment of our relationship, and soon all the Keitas in Moribabougou were dropping by for their cola nuts and a chance the meet their prospective cousin. Birama came with us to break the glad news to Balamine, and the old man glowed with pleasure. "I told you to take a wife," he said. As we were leaving, he called Birama aside for a private word.

Back at my parents' house there was another confidential chat, this time between Birama and Mariam, and then the two of them led Aisha and me on a long walk, walking slowly because Birama's legs were hurting him. We passed through the village, skirted a small swamp, and came eventually to an untended field three or four acres in size, surrounded by a low, broken cement wall. A few dry stalks of millet were scattered here and there among the scrub trees and the brown weeds, and a tiny finger of the river trickled alongside. I was probably wrong, but it seems to me now that there were tears in Birama's eyes as he spoke. Aisha translated, but I found her lack of enthusiasm embarrassing.

"This is Birama's field. Actually, it is Balamine's but he has given it to Birama to farm. Balamine has many fields, but he does not have enough sons to work all of them, and Birama is too weak for farming. You can see the con-

65

dition of the land. Birama says that if you will move to Moribabougou, he will let you use it for your own farm. The land is good, and all year there is water." There was a long pause as I tried to digest this extraordinary offer. Aisha kept looking at the ground. Mariam evidently sensed my qualms about beginning a new career as an African farmer.

"If you don't want to farm," she said, "you can make a restaurant."

True to form, Aisha said not a word on the way back, and I was just as glad. My mind was overwhelmed by the magnificence of Birama's offer—Balamine's, really, for such a rich present could only have been given by the family chief.

Naturally, I was flattered—how could I not be?—a stranger from another culture so thoroughly accepted into this African family that he was invited to share its land. Of course, this land would not actually be mine to dispose of as I pleased. In the traditional Malian village, no one "owns" the land. What one does own is the right to use it and to enjoy its fruits and to pass those rights down to one's heirs and to their heirs, *ad perpetuum,* the land itself remains the possession of the family. It is the most significant gift a cash-poor Malian farmer can give.

Why had Balamine made it? Well, first of all, affection. Earlier he had offered me a wife from his family, and now he was inviting me to share the family land. Certainly these were gestures of love, and I don't want to diminish them because of my own false modesty. Yes, this was above all a gift of love.

But Balamine and Birama had practical reasons, too. The land was good and potentially arable, but it was now degenerating into scrub and brush because of years of disuse. Birama, who had the usage of the land, was unable to work it and had no cash to hire labor or to buy equipment or even seeds. I, too, was old, but my frequent bicycle trips from Bamako must have made me appear stronger. Anyway, I don't think that either Balamine or Birama expected me to cultivate the field myself. This would take a small squad of husky young laborers, and maybe even a plow, all of which I might provide along with a badly needed pump for dry-season irrigation.

And finally there was now Aisha. Mariam and Birama had no children, and Birama was apparently impotent. When they saw me wooing a strong young African woman, they hoped that this problem, too, might be solved.

Aisha wasn't silent, though, when we reached the house. "You a farmer!" she burst out. "What an *insult!* Doesn't Balamine understand that you are an *intellectual*—a *professor?* Yes, I know you think he was being kind, but really he was *insulting* you! How could you ever be happy in a *village?*

66

"Aisha, we could be very happy in Moribabougou," I insisted.

"Not as happy as in New Jersey," she replied.

In my heart of hearts, I also knew that the offer was one I couldn't accept, but I also knew that the making of it was a very large thing and I couldn't reject it out of hand. Patiently I went back over the reasons why we couldn't afford to live in America.

As I should have predicted, Aisha simply didn't believe me. If I were young, she might have. It was normal for young men, even young American men, to be poor; they were just starting life. But an old American man without the means to support a wife in his own wealthy country—this was a contradiction no Malian could accept. Certainly none of my students could, nor my fellow teachers, nor my families in Moribabougou and Bamako. Nor could Aisha. She was sure I was trying to deceive her.

"But we can be very happy in Africa," I repeated.

"Not so happy as in America," she countered, and the conversation hobbled to a halt. There seemed no way to convince her I was telling the truth.

67

7

God in the Classroom and
Other Anecdotes

When I got back to classes after my long, slow summer, I found that I had at last been given my favorite subject to teach, nineteenth century American literature, as well as black American literature, which I had taught the year before. What a treat it was to encourage these young Moslems, still struggling to master English verb forms, to stretch their capacities to understand writers like Thoreau, Emerson, and Whitman, who believed that truth was to be found, not in the rituals and dogma of organized religion, but in one's own limitless soul! Stretched my own capacities too, for I found myself obliged to define all the terms of the discussion—not just "transcendentalism" and "oversoul," but even more common words like God, Man, and Nature.

This was not easy, for how does one explain Emerson's belief in the preeminence of personal intuition, his faith in the dogma Trust Thyself, to young men and women whose every thought has heretofore been bent to fit the tight measures of custom and tradition? Generally, I found that the essay "Self-

Reliance" was about as much as my students could digest, because of its mind-shaking thesis that God was within them all and that therefore the "true man" had no need of ministers, priests, imams, or other intermediaries to interpret for him the will of God.

Of course, I tried scrupulously to avoid taking a position in the lively discussions that arose from such ideas, but simply presented the views of the writers as best I could. Nevertheless, there was in every class section a small coterie of Muslim fundamentalists who were angered at the very idea that they must read the works of men who minimized tradition and encouraged independent thinking. One such student accused me of atheism because Emerson often used the word Nature when he was clearly talking about God. Fortunately, such students were in the great minority, and some of these seemed to come around to the understanding that there was nothing wrong with noticing that not every farmer planted his field with the same crops his father had.

Once during a discussion of "Self-Reliance," Ousmane Traorè, who at six feet four or five was the tallest Malian I saw in all my years in the country, wondered if there might be a conflict between the Emersonian ideal of indi-vidualism and the American ideal of equality. The rugged individualism of the pioneer may once have been a positive force in promotion of equality, he pointed out, but the selfish individualism of Jay Gould and the other rob-ber barons of the nineteenth century undermined it. Ousmane later won a scholarship to the United States and, while he was there, visited Concord and Walden Pond with my sister Nancy. He has since become an instructor at ENSup.

Mark Twain was another favorite of the students, though we had neither the books nor the time to tackle major works like *Tom Sawyer* or *Huckleberry Finn*. Instead, we made do with brief selections from *Life on the Mississippi*. One day the text led us to into a discussion of one of my own concerns, the preservation of innocence, that childlike sense of wonder that makes the world seem each day new and therefore exciting. In the passage, Twain tells how he began his apprenticeship as a Mississippi River pilot "in a speechless rapture," filled with awe at the unpredictable beauty of the river. Finally, though, he learns to read the river, not as "a book with pretty pictures in it," but as "the grimmest and most dead-earnest of reading matter." But this mas-tery of the river has been at dreadful cost. "I had lost something which could never be restored to me while I lived. All the grace, the beauty, the poetry, had gone out of the majestic river!"

We talked loosely about the jading effect of experience and whether the loss of wonder and delight was inevitable. Mamadou Cissoko, a thirty-five-year-old former grade-school teacher who could always be counted on to penetrate to the kernel of a discussion, pointed out that Twain, while he was telling us that he had lost the poetry of the river, was actually recreating it in his prose. This led us to consider that one of the most important functions of imaginative literature is to do just that, to reawaken our capacity for delight, to shock us into a momentary return to innocence.

All this led to a half-time pep talk on behalf of poetry and fiction, which most of the students were wondering why they must study at all.

Madinè

A few days before the opening of school, a second granddaughter came to live with Fanta, and she, too, quickly entered into the routine. Madinè was starting kindergarten, and what a delightful contrast to her older sister! Ami was serious and sober; Madinè was a fireball. She talked incessantly and, when she wasn't talking, she laughed. She had a gait as swift and graceful as a gazelle's, and I often challenged her to races just so I could watch her long, easy strides—not at all like a child's, more like the form of an Olympic champion. Each morning after a breakfast of bread and coffee on my back steps, she would follow Ami on the three-kilometer walk to school, and each evening she would return with her for "homework." As far as I could tell, Madinè's homework consisted of coloring geometrical objects and drawing squiggly lines, but Ami would watch her intently, sometimes scolding, as if this were Madinè's most important duty in the world. Once, Ami brought along a small switch of leaves and swatted Madinè with it every time the child started nodding off to sleep. Then, when Madinè buried her face for a moment in her work, Ami would give me a broad grin. In spite of this sisterly support, Madinè inevitably fell asleep before her work was done and, when Ami had finished her own homework, I carried the little one home. I had acquired another family.

Mamady

By now I had become so thoroughly at ease with my students, and they with me, that I was sometimes trapped into the comfortable conviction that our cultural differences were superficial—skin deep. Many of them were and are, but others are profound, imprinted by centuries of tradition—African tradition, Islamic tradition, western tradition—and they can be bridged only by love and will.

Mamady Kouyatè was a Malian version of Jimmy Stewart, a lean, long-limbed, good-looking young man in the third year who spoke with a drawl so

70

thick and so nasal you would think he had learned his English listening to the sound track of *Mr. Smith Goes to Washington*. He came by one evening to talk to me about the *mémoire* he must write next year and to ask me to supervise it. He had heard I was planning to come back.

Mamady was as lethargic as he looked and sounded. At least that was the impression he had given me in class; I wasn't even sure he would pass the year. The topic he proposed, "Sin in the Works of Nathaniel Hawthorne," had been covered twice before and was therefore automatically ineligible. Anyway, I felt that literary analysis was well beyond Mamady's capacities and steered him instead to a study of American foreign policy toward Africa since World War II, for which a lot of material was available at the U.S.I.S. library. I also explained that I was already overcommitted and couldn't handle another *mémoire*. Mamady accepted this cheerfully, and somehow the conversation turned to his personal life. He was eager to talk about it.

He had formed a sadly doomed relationship with one of the brightest students in the class, a tall, shy, good-looking girl named Mati Traorè. I say "doomed," not because of the disparity in their abilities, but because her family name was Traorè and his was Kouyatè, and therefore they could never marry. This was no ordinary, or even extraordinary, family feud like the Montagues and the Capulets. The taboo on marriage between the Kouyatès and the Traorès goes back six hundred years, perhaps longer, at any rate for as long as the oral histories of the West African peoples have existed. For, from the heyday of the great Empire of Mali, the Traorès, like the Keitas, had been nobles, and the Kouyatès had been commoners, "men of caste." The name Kouyatè signified that Mamady was a griot, a minstrel, and therefore inferior.

Now this was truly ironic for, if it were not for the griots who sang their praises, no one here would know who on earth the Traorès were. Over the centuries, the griots of West Africa recorded and glorified in their songs and stories the heroic deeds of the nobles who employed them, and then faithfully passed these histories down to their descendants, from generation to generation. Like Homer in ancient Greece, they were the poets, the historians, the bards of their societies, and it is thanks to them that today the most illiterate Malian knows more about his country than many Americans know about their own. Yet Mamady, because he bore the griot name of Kouyatè, could never marry his classmate Mati Traorè.

"What will happen if you marry?" I asked.

"She will be put out of her family. Her father will never permit her in the house again."

71

"But how can that be? I know the President of Mali is a Traorè, but so are some of the poorest farmers in the country and the most miserable beggars in the city. What can be more noble than a poet?"

"A Traorè," said Mamady in his characteristically laconic way. "Or a Keita. We are their paid entertainers."

"Are you yourself a griot?" I asked, incredulously, because I couldn't imagine Mamady writing a coherent paragraph in any language whatever, let alone an epic poem.

He smiled wryly. "I'm not even a good singer. My grandfather was a griot, and his ancestors before him. So, according to Mati's family, I am just an entertainer, a juggler, not good for a noblewoman's husband."

Griots are not the only men of caste in Mali. Blacksmiths, weavers, hunters, fishermen, in fact the followers of most non-pastoral or military occupations, fall into the same social category. A few months earlier, Aisha had shown me a melodramatic little story she had written on the theme. As a child, the daughter of a farmer had as friend and playmate the son of a *forgeron*, a blacksmith. Now, in the countryside the blacksmith is a man of some importance, for he not only makes the tools and wagons that every farmer needs, but he is also a sculptor and carves the ceremonial masks and idols which bring good harvests and many sons to the people of his village. Often he has more money than the farmer, but he is nevertheless an inferior, a man of caste.

After primary school, according to Aisha's story, the children were sent off to live with relatives in larger towns so they could continue their schooling, and they became separated. Years later, they met again as university students in the big city, and they fell in love. The girl's father, when he heard of his daughter's attachment to the son of a blacksmith, was outraged and sent her to live with an uncle in a far part of the country. The young man followed her and they married. Loyal to the traditions of his people, the uncle killed him with a gun.

"Would your family behave like that if you married someone from the blacksmith caste?" I asked her at the time.

"Of course," she answered. "It is the custom of our people. It is like a law."

"And if you marry an American? Will they drive you out?"

Aisha wasn't happy with my question. "Don't worry yourself about such silly things," she'd said.

I looked now at Mamady who was leaning back in his chair, long legs stretched out, looking marvelously like a TV cowboy or a Graduate Fellow at Harvard and staring pensively at the ceiling; he should have been sucking on a blade of grass or an unlit pipe. "Is there nothing whatever you can do?" I asked him.

"There is one thing we are thinking of. If we have two children together without being married—two children, not only one—they will have to permit the marriage. That, too, is the custom. We are thinking about that."

I took a closer look at Mamady. His dilemma was real enough, but his manner seemed much too easygoing for a lover in such soul-wracking circumstances. I would have been more impressed if he had shown a little less cool, if he had kneaded his fingers or paced the room as I imagined Mati would have done if it had been she who was telling me the story. Griot or no, Mamady didn't look like good husband material to me.

"Mamady, do yourself a favor," I told him. "I like Mati and I like you, too. If you really care for each other, you'd better give some time to your studies. Think about what will happen to the two of you if you fail while she passes. And this could happen."

Boubacar and Dho

When I began teaching in Mali, I was awed by the problem of communicating with my students. I couldn't understand their English, and I was seldom sure they understood mine. Now, nearly two years later, I found myself marveling that their English was as good as it was. As children they had grown up speaking Bambara or one of six or eight other indigenous languages, and this was still the language they spoke at home and in the market. When they entered school, their instruction was in French, which is the official language of the country. English, then, was their *third* language, and learning it couldn't have been easy for any of them. I've complained about the lack of sufficient textbooks at ENSup, but there were no English textbooks at all in most of the lycées—just reading passages one or two paragraphs in length, typed and badly mimeographed on individual sheets of paper; everything else was written on the blackboard, and the students copied it neatly into their notebooks. In any case, few students had access to electric light so, in the rare instances when homework was assigned, it had to be done during the daylight hours, or else in a public place.

For serious students, the problem was especially acute. Hardly any bookstores carried works in English, and the British and American films shown in the open-air theaters all had sound tracks dubbed in French. Their one useful resource was the modest library of the American Cultural Center, run by the U.S. Information Service, plus the Center's occasional films and visiting speakers. And, of course, our little English Club at ENSup. Amazingly, most students seemed to overcome these awesome handicaps. By the time they reached their third or fourth year at ENSup, almost everyone could read, write, speak, and understand English well enough to get along. A handful were brilliant.

I'm thinking in particular of two students whose *mémoires* I supervised during my second year at ENSup. Boubacar Belco Diallo was the "creative genius" of the class, with ambitions to make a name for himself as a playwright. Throughout the year, while earning an A average in his classes and serving as the English Club's first president, Boubacar managed to write, direct, and choreograph an entire musical production—in French and Bambara—for the *Biennale*, the country's nationwide arts competition, and the short play he wrote as part of this show won first prize for drama. For his *mémoire*, Boubacar wrote about "protest" in the black American theater, and somehow managed to find, read, and analyze more than a dozen plays by writers like Wright, Baldwin, Hansbury and Baraka.

Boubacar's greatest problem was his glibness; his mind sprayed out words and ideas as rapidly as a machine gun, often without taking time to aim. He ended up with a stunning *mémoire*, but on the way learned the meaning of the word "bullshit," which I scrawled over many of his pages of empty rhetoric.

I had known Boubacar would do well. Dho Konè, though, was a surprise. Dho was a tall, powerfully built Bobo from Burkina Faso who looked as though he should really be playing tight end for the New York Giants instead of struggling to become an underpaid English teacher. During my first year in Mali, Dho was in two of my classes, composition and black American literature, and in both he was painstaking and deliberate. He made few mistakes but no brilliancies either, and I put him down as a capable plodder. How wrong I was! If Boubacar's mind was like a machine gun, Dho's was like a cannon. He took a lot of time aiming at what he wanted to hit, but then, Boom! During our studies of Frederick Douglass, Dho had become fascinated with the institution of slavery, and he chose as his topic, "The Daily Life of an American Slave." Dho's *mémoire* had no frills, no paeans to freedom, no impassioned diatribes on the horrors of slavery such as Boubacar might have included—just a powerful mass of fact and anecdote, painstakingly researched, brilliantly organized, and clearly presented. Like Boubacar, Dho was awarded the highest possible grade, 15.

The Joys and Perils of Routine

When I was young, I had a phobia about routine. I think it came from my father who, after years of adventuresome struggle against poverty, found himself "trapped," as he put it, in the suburban routine—catching the same commuter train to the city each morning, doing the same job each day, taking the same dreary train home each evening. The fact that his job was varied and interesting, and that he was good at it, made no difference; to him it was a "squirrel cage," which revolved the faster he ran, so that he remained always in the same place and his progress was always an illusion.

I had for a while this same fear of being caught up in "the system," whatever that was. I remember a time in my late twenties when I took my first and only job with a big corporation, as editor of the Shell Oil Company's house organ, *Shell News*. I was sitting in the office of the personnel director and we had just concluded the necessary business about salary and so on. He leaned back in his enormous chair and, in a conspiratorial manner and with a thin smile I have decided in retrospect was sincere, expounded at length the details of the company's retirement program—the truly marvelous benefits I would receive after thirty-odd years of service. I remember how hard I tried to look interested, and how heartsick I really was. Today, I know how much I benefit from routine—a standard wake-up time, a schedule of classes, the necessary coordination of cooking and eating. It is comforting to know that, in small things at least, there is a dependable pattern to my existence, that there are decisions which have been made once and for all, and that I am now free to experience other things.

I found that even my relations with Aisha were falling into a pattern. I saw her, without open acknowledgment, in my classes on Monday and Tuesday mornings, and on Saturday afternoons she came to the house for one of our chaste, though increasingly intimate, conversations.

Alas, the everyday kindness of routine sets seductive traps, and we must all of us be forever wary. One afternoon about the time of our American Thanksgiving, I received my comeuppance.

For some days I had noticed an English-speaking African hanging out in the courtyard of the Peace Corps, trying to engage volunteers in conversation. I spoke with him once or twice and found he was from the English-speaking country of Ghana and had no special business here in Mali, certainly not with the Peace Corps. I took him to be a moocher and was never more than cordial. On this one day, I was waiting to see the Director about extending my service for another year when he sat down beside me on one of the cushioned bamboo chairs outside the office. He wanted to talk about his troubles, and I was obliged to listen.

A sad but interesting man—a journalist without a country—a refugee with a six-month UN passport because his own country wouldn't give a passport of its own—a sick and lonely intellectual whose English would be good enough to get him a job in an English-speaking country but was useless to him here where he could speak barely a word of French and needed an interpreter just to get around. And of course his lack of papers was a continuing problem.

As he talked, it seemed to me that he needed most of all someone who could give him practical help—money, a job, a place to stay. He dreamed impossibly of going to the United States for graduate work in journalism, to Paris for medical treatment for a chronic ailment, to any place in the world where he could use the language and the writing skills he'd learned in Ghana and, later in his wanderings, in Liberia.

His story troubled me, made me uncomfortable with myself for my inability and unwillingness to help, and made me in consequence irritated with him. I was relieved when my turn came to see the Director and I could end this little ordeal with a handshake and a cluck of sympathy.

When I came out, the Ghanaian was still there. Alone. I greeted him and walked to the gate. He followed.

"Where are you going?" I asked him, not out of curiosity but to forestall any attempt to follow me to my house.

"I don't know," he said, and I stood still while he walked slowly off in the general direction of downtown. He didn't look back but kept walking on, head bent, shoulders drooping, growing smaller and smaller until at last he turned a corner and was gone.

But what could I have done? There was no way I could have helped him find a job, even if he knew French, and it would have made no sense to encourage him. A handout was out of the question, and anyhow, he hadn't asked for one, did not in fact seem totally broke. Why should I concern myself so? Then it occurred to me that I might have given him a little warmth, a little comradeship. The man was lost, friendless, his future blank, his past rubbed out. I could have talked with him for a while. Or let him talk. Why hadn't I?

The answer was obvious. I hadn't wanted to get involved, hadn't wanted to complicate my smoothly flowing life with some kind of hapless hanger-on. I had built up such a comforting routine—breakfasts with Fanta and her grandchildren, classes every Monday, Tuesday, and Wednesday morning—supervising student-teachers on Thursdays and Fridays—Bambara lessons twice a week with Nèguèdougou—visits from Aisha every Saturday afternoon—and every evening letters to write and books to read. This fellow could be a leech.

Still, the memory of his frail silhouette shrinking out of sight down the road stayed with me like the image of the Little Tramp walking splayfooted into the distance just after losing job, Paulette Goddard, and every shred of hope. I remembered that he had mentioned being a Catholic, finding sustenance by attending mass on Sundays. I mounted my bike and rode downtown to the cathedral.

There, the black sexton took me to the office of Father Maurice, a lean, stoop-shouldered Frenchman of about fifty, perfectly cast as the colonial

76

priest. Yes, he knew such a man; his name was Arthur, and he came regularly to mass. Did I have a job for him? No, no job, no money either. I just thought he might like to talk with someone in his own language, to share some tea or some food. I left a written invitation to lunch the following Sunday, and now I felt both better and worse.

During the days following, I met another African passing through Bamako—an aspiring poet from Togo named Emanuel Agbenou. Somehow, Emanuel had been given my name as a person to look up in Mali, so I invited him to come over for tea at ten o'clock Sunday morning, the same day Arthur was expected later for lunch. Emanuel spoke no English and, while my French was now good enough for ordinary conversations, I didn't have much confidence in my ability to cope intelligently with French poetry, so I invited Nèguèdougou to join us. Nèguè knew everything.

This turned out to be a right idea. Emanuel, it seemed, wrote poems specifically for young people; he was in Mali to scout out opportunities to read them to the local equivalent of junior high schools. He read a few of his poems to us in a highly oratorical style that reminded me of Voznesenski or some other Russian poet reading his work on public television in the U.S. The language was direct, the rhythms strong, and the thoughts expressed were very, very long. The later Wordsworth would have loved him and so, Nèguè and I agreed, would the junior-high-school students of Mali. Nèguè, who not only knew everything, but could arrange everything also, made a date to meet Emanuel on Wednesday at his new office at the Institut Pédagogique National. He was going to line up an opportunity for Emanuel to read his poems around the country.

At some time while all this was going on, Arthur arrived, an hour early. Since he spoke no French, and the others no English, I found myself in the unexpected position of interlocutor and translator for three Africans from three different countries—Togo, Mali, and Ghana. I like role-playing, and I played this role to the hilt—the affable, culturally awakened, bilingual host.

When Fanta arrived with lunch, Emanuel and Nèguè took this as their cue to leave, giving Arthur and me the chance to talk together in English. I wanted Arthur to tell me of his problems with censorship in Ghana and with the new military government of Liberia, but he was more concerned with the "mysterious things" that had been happening to him—how his family in Ghana unexpectedly turned against him; how he discovered himself suddenly penniless in Liberia, with all his property and savings gone; how impossible it was for him to know what was bad luck and what was his own fault. He had obviously been well prepared to accept his personal guilt, but he was deeply bothered by the possibility that he might, after all, be innocent. I learned little about Ghana and about Liberia, and not a great deal I could understand about Arthur. I invited him to come back in a month for another visit, but I never heard from him again.

A Second Visit to the *Marabout*

It was early March, in the heart of the dry season when the mango tree produces its choicest and ripest fruits. On every branch of the three huge mango trees in my yard, the heavy green-and-yellow, fruits, shaped like small footballs, dangled in clusters from long green tendrils, and almost every day Fanta and Ami, and sometimes one of Ami's older sisters, would reach up into the trees with long bamboo poles tipped with homemade hooks of bent wire and knock down basketsful of the ripest. The poles were at least fifteen feet long, but still the women could reach less than a third of the way up, so Nèguè would come over sometimes to help. He would climb barefoot and as nimbly as any denizen of the jungle, and he would bring down in half an hour as many mangoes as Fanta and her grandchildren could gather in an afternoon. When he was called to Mopti for a week to help bury an uncle, the ripening fruits kept turning from green to yellow, orange, and bright vermilion, like the leaves of maples. I decided I was still young enough to climb up myself.

Mango trees, even big ones, are fairly easy to climb. The larger branches are well spaced and slope upward at a gentle angle—twenty-five to thirty degrees at most—and there are very few small shoots or leafy branches in the center of the tree to get in a climber's way. They remind me of the maple trees I used to climb as a boy during summers in Vermont.

I felt like such a boy now. While Fanta protested vehemently, I borrowed a short iron ladder from next door and, with just a little difficulty, swung a leg and then the rest of my body onto the lowest branch. Ami handed me the wire-tipped pole, and I mounted further. How simple it seemed! Secure in my sneakers, I was able to walk—literally to walk—the length of several of the largest branches.

Handling the long, heavy pole was more difficult, but before my arms tired I was able to bring down a couple of dozen of the ripest-looking fruits. Then I dropped the bamboo and started down.

There was nothing tricky about the descent until I reached the lowest branch. Then I realized with dismay that hoisting myself from the ladder to the branch had been a lot easier than swinging myself back down from the branch to the ladder was going to be. I wrapped both arms around the branch and clung to it, while my right foot groped blindly for the topmost rung. But I had overestimated my strength. Within seconds, my nearly two hundred pounds proved too much for my old and tired arms to support and, to the shrill screams of Fanta and Ami, I fell crashing to the paving stones.

I was lucky. I was well bruised, and the insides of my arms were scraped from wrist to shoulder, but there were no apparent breaks or sprains. I did have one scare. While checking my scrapes, I noticed that the large vein on my left forearm had popped right out of its place, and was protruding, in a kind of skin-covered loop, almost a quarter inch from my arm. Quickly, before Fanta could see it, I pushed the loop down with my forefinger, and miraculously it stayed in place.

When I told Nèguè later about this fresh sign of physical degeneration, his first thought was of my romance with Aisha. He pursed his lips disapprovingly and suggested another visit to his friend Mama, the *marabout*, this time for a potion to insure my virility.

"But Nèguè," I argued, "I'm not going to get married for at least a year. And Aisha will never have sex before marriage, she says that."

"Don't believe it. You can never trust a woman. And don't be ashamed, either. It is common for old men to prepare themselves."

The three of us sat lotuslike on the mattress, and I watched Mama write rows of Arabic characters in ink on a thin slab of unpainted wood.

"He is copying passages from the Qur'an," Nèguè explained. "About love and procreation."

Mama now picked up a large jug and poured water slowly over the lettered slab. The water drained into another jug below, washing the slab clean. In the second jug I could now see suspended tiny flecks of jet. Mama spoke, and Nèguè translated.

"Tomorrow, you must buy a gift for twins. Shoes, toys, baby clothes—anything. Then give them to the first mother of twins you meet." He saw my puzzlement. "Don't worry. The mothers know that twins are a powerful charm. They will approach you in the market. Afterwards, go home and mix a little of this potion—maybe a spoonful—with a glass of tamarind juice. Then drink. And do this every day."

The next day, I went to the market and bought two identical white T-shirts imprinted with pictures of the Empire State Building. Almost immediately, I was besieged by three women with twins; two of the women carried their babies strapped to their backs; the third, whose twins were older, was towing them in a child's red wagon. I cheerfully admired all six infants and gave the shirts to the mother with the wagon, since they would fit her children better. Back home, I took the potion from the refrigerator and was about to prepare it when I realized that the water had come from the river by Mama's house, and was almost certainly polluted. I took a moment to admire the mystical black flecks dancing in the jug; then I poured the rejuvenating magic down the drain.

79

Fanta's Cooking Makes the News

Vice-President Bush had been touring Africa as a prelude to announcing new American aid, and the Peace Corps in Bamako was on his list of stops. To demonstrate to him Peace Corps' program for improving wood stoves, it was decided to ask a Malian woman to prepare a meal of the national dish—*tow,* or millet mush with sauce.

Fanta, whose cooking had become known among volunteers because of my hospitality, was selected for the honor. She cooked up a really fabulous dish with two traditional sauces—a red sauce of meat and tomato, and a green sauce made with okra. Because she hadn't been cleared by the Secret Service, she wasn't allowed to attend the ceremonial tasting but photographers took dozens of pictures of the Vice President grinning with professional delight as he tasted Fanta's version of the Malian national dish, and one of these made page one of the *Washington Post.*

I showed the clipping to Fanta, thinking she would be pleased. Instead, she was furious. She had been the principal contributor to a news event of world importance—and for the price of an ordinary meal.

I had earlier applied for a third year in the Peace Corps so I could be on hand when Aisha finished school, and this entitled me to a six-week home leave in the U.S. Mama Coulibaly, one of Peace Corps' many Malian employees, drove me to the plane and Nèguèdougou came along to see me off. He professed astonishment at Aisha's absence.

"She said she was afraid she would cry," I told him. He scoffed at my naiveté. "And do you believe her?"

8

Dreams and Near Disasters

W hat a busy place America is! I'm not thinking only of the visible and audible busyness—the hurrying traffic, the crowded elevators, the jets roaring overhead, the events and pseudo-events that crowd the pages of the Times. I'm thinking of the lives of ordinary people, people I know. As I saw them now after two years in a wholly different world, they seemed preoccupied, even my closest friends, with keeping busy, keeping "productive." At its worst, this passion for busyness meant filling every moment with some kind of activity, however needless or inane—sipping, snacking, shopping, watching television, doing crosswords on the toilet.

But even at its best, where the low goal of keeping busy was replaced by the higher one of living a full life, it looked to me that this full life was in danger of becoming too full. Many of my most estimable friends behaved like hyperkinetic Renaissance people: they swam, they jogged, they took courses, they painted, they worked late—anything to spare themselves from a moment free for idleness, loneliness, or reflection.

Certainly, too much loneliness is a terrible thing, and there have been years when I've been intolerant of even a small bit of it. But I know now that none of the marvels that continue to illuminate my life could have entered without it.

My Peace Corps colleagues had warned me of "reverse culture shock," a stomach-turning reaction to America's supermarket society after years of simple living in a poor country, and of the hazards of too much rich food after a diet of mostly rice.

I had neither of these problems. My son Wally had thoughtfully arranged for the two of us to spend my first week of leave in my brother's vacant cottage on the Maine coast. There, we were isolated from television and even radio. I spent my days fishing, reading, and making phone calls. We ate well but simply; one afternoon we bought a pair of lobsters from a boatman who was emptying his traps at the edge of the dock and boiled them up for dinner; once we went out to a restaurant for chowder, fish and french fries. Out of former habit I bought a copy of the *New York Times* on my first Sunday back, and I was surprised at how little I found that interested me. Its magnitude seemed pretentious and vulgar, generated not by the importance of its news stories, but by the aggressiveness of its advertisers and the self-absorption of its readers.

All in all, it was a refreshing trip home. I visited my daughters Amy and Linda in Staten Island and Connecticut, visited family and old friends all over the northeast, and even picked up three hundred dollars for reading my poetry at the University of Massachusetts. Everywhere I went I showed the handful of photographs I'd been able to take with borrowed cameras. The family was especially interested in the pictures of Aisha, whom I described vaguely as "a special friend"; one of these photos showed her in a preppy American outfit which my eldest daughter Linda had sent her as a present. There were no hackneyed reactions to her blackness, but most of my family, especially my brother, seemed embarrassed by her youth.

Dreams of Greatness

Two weeks after the beginning of the fall term at ENSup, the Ministry of Education asked the school's director for recommendations on the curriculum of a "University of Mali," a project that had been sitting on the drawing board for twenty years, with no visible result but the minutes of a few committee meetings. I was named to a new committee, along with senior members of the French, Russian, German, history, psychology, mathematics, and science departments, to come up with some ideas.

No one of us believed in the reality of the project, but the school Director begged us to take it seriously, as a matter of form and to help him keep his job.

Certainly, Mali could use a university. Higher education came to Mali from France as a kind of vocational training to develop the teachers, accountants, surveyors, tax collectors, postal clerks, and other professional and bureaucratic personnel the empire needed to keep the colony running. After independence in 1960, the vocational emphasis remained, but Mali's leaders believed that the country also needed an intelligentsia—a cadre of more highly, more broadly, more *liberally* educated men and women to replace the ousted French masters. Up to the present, this has meant sending the country's potential leaders to universities abroad, fostering a continued dependence on the great powers and an emphasis on what is called here "European" culture. And so the concept of a Malian national university was born.

But the project never got off the ground. This was partly because of the Ministry's inertia and lack of leadership: Many well-placed bureaucrats had strongly vested interests in the programs as they were. But mostly, there just wasn't any money, and the Ministry's "promise-everything-do-nothing" reputation hadn't inspired a rush of contributions from the donor countries.

Now the military government had revived the project—but in a way that made it more remote than ever.

Frightened at the possibility of another student-faculty strike like that of 1981-1982, the ministers decided against the establishment of a single, centralized university in a major city like Bamako, Segou, or Sikasso, and elected instead to break up the intellectual phalanx into six schools, each in a different region. The School of Arts and Letters, with which we ENSup professors were to be affiliated, was planned for Timbuktoo, romantically described in the Ministry's official announcement as "the mysterious city." I was momentarily bewitched.

Four years earlier, when I first learned I was to teach English with the Peace Corps in Mali, I had rushed over to the Hackensack, New Jersey, public library to look up the country on a map of Africa. The first thing my eyes fixed on was not the size or the shape or the location of the country, but the single word "Timbuktoo" printed in small, bold-faced type beside a tiny black dot where the green land ended and the pale yellow of the desert began.

I remembered the name from my childhood reading, for Timbuktoo once marked for Europeans the end of the known world, the remote destination of caravans from the north, the farthest reach of white traders and explorers toward the dark regions of Africa. But Timbuktoo was not only a destination. It was a beginning—a point of entry into another world mysterious and unknown. Expressions of remoteness and incredible distance leaped to mind—expressions like "from here to Timbuktoo" and "all the way to Timbuktoo." Where had I read them? Richard Haliburton? Rudyard Kipling? Why did the name resonate in my memory like Persepolis, Xanadu, Camelot,

Asgard, and Eden—all those glorious lost places of legend and belief? And now I knew that this place at least was real. It was actually on the map, in a distant part of the country where I would be working, and I resolved that I must go there.

Since that dazzling hour in the library, I received many portents urging me to make that journey. The most powerful of these was during my "baptismal" ceremony in Moribabougou, when the newly named Namory Keita danced to the beat of tom-toms and, like Laurens van der Post, felt the ancient rhythms of Africa surging in his veins. My newly bestowed ancestors had been the original emperors of Mali; their wealth in gold had almost destroyed the economy of the Near East; the center of learning they founded at the edge of the Sahara became the fabled city of Timbuktoo. And now I was being asked to help plan a new university on that legendary site. Heady stuff.

Legendary or not, the plan was in fact nonsense, and not a single member of our select committee could believe it would ever be implemented. Timbuktoo was a long day's trip from Bamako, longer from some other cities. It had no electricity, no reliable supply of drinking water. Centuries of encroachment by the desert had separated it from its original life-line, the river Niger, and so robbed it of its commercial reason for being. Passengers and freight bound for Timbuktoo by river now had to be offloaded at Dire, almost twenty kilometers south, and to finish their journeys by truck or taxi. In any case, the steamers could navigate the river during only three months of the year.

What was left of Timbuktoo was the legend, and this was powerfully imprinted, not only in Malian, but in European folklore. Almost every visitor to Mali takes a side trip to "the mysterious city." Most of my colleagues on the committee had themselves visited Timbuktoo as a way of paying homage to the past. Yet not one of them wanted to live and work there.

Nèguèdougou was aghast at the Ministry's proposal and cried out almost in pain, "The only thing I can understand is that somebody in the government wants to get even richer by putting up a lot of new buildings no one will ever use. Do you have any idea how rich some of these officials are? Of course not. No one knows, because they and their cousins keep all their money in Switzerland; they don't know how to spend it all. Look at the way their wives dress! They have more shoes than that woman in the Philippines, Imelda Marcos. And still they keep grasping out for more!"

What made Nèguè angriest was not the greed of these officials. He could have accepted that. It was their lack of faith in Mali. "They could use all this money to help develop their country. They could build dams and factories and roads. There is gold here. Why don't these government big shots invest some of their money to dig mines, instead of giving all the concessions to foreigners? I'll tell you why. They think the whole country is going down the drain anyway, so they might as well grab what's left while they can. There are no patriots in this country."

Nègùe was exaggerating. I had got to know many proud and patriotic Malians. Nègùe himself was profoundly patriotic. And not just for his own country but for all of Africa. "People have to be proud of being Malians, proud of being Africans," he had said. He felt that the one hope for Africa to catch up with the rest of the world was to break down the artificial barriers between French-speaking and English-speaking cultures and to foster a culture and an economy that was continent-wide." Like America. Or even Europe.

"Instead of this crazy dream of making a university to teach a European-style curriculum in Timbuktoo, why not an institute of *African* studies right here in Bamako? Or in Sikasso or Segou? Our people don't need to memorize the birthdates of the kings of France. They need to know the histories, the politics, the economies of all our sister countries in Africa. They need to study African geography, African literature, African economics. African resources."

Nègùe was really high on this and I wished he were telling it to some of Mali's politicians, or to the country as a whole on one of his Sunday morning radio broadcasts on education. But of course those broadcasts were subject to Ministry approval.

"Do you know," he went on, "that there is no school of African studies anywhere on the continent. We could attract students from Senegal, from Nigeria, from Kenya, from all over Africa. Students from French-speaking countries would have to learn English. Students from English-speaking countries would have to learn French. It could be a famous school, a truly *African* university. And right here in Mali."

Drought and Disease

Meanwhile, the poor country was having other problems. Bush volunteers returning to Bamako for Thanksgiving were bringing with them the first trustworthy reports of the drought in the north and of the mass exodus of families from the stricken areas bordering the desert. The catastrophe was real—both more serious and less dramatic than had apparently been represented on television and in newspapers back in America. Moors, Songhais, Tuaregs, Fulani, and other nomadic and seminomadic peoples from the Sahel, and some of the poorer families from Timbuktoo, Gao and other population centers on the shore of the desert were fleeing from their homelands into makeshift refugee camps set up in provincial capitals and larger towns to the south. A few bought their animals with them, but most left them dead or dying behind.

85

Emergency rations of rice were dispatched and most of it, my friends told me, got through to the people who needed it, though every volunteer had his own sickening stories to tell of venality and corruption.

Far more disturbing than the immediate famine was the outlook for the future. Hundreds of thousands of cattle and sheep, sorely needed to replenish herds and flocks already depleted by the great drought often years before, died or were sold away in panic. Seed grain that should have been saved for planting during the next rainy season was being eaten now. One more bad year and the streets of Bamako would be filled with light-skinned Tuaregs and their black-veiled wives, turbaned Moors and wiry Fulani with their shepherds' staffs and knee-length pantaloons. What they might do for work, no one knew.

Everyone I spoke with agreed that the misguided hand of man—his over-planting and overgrazing of this fragile land—was to a large extent responsible for what was happening. A few said that man was almost entirely responsible and that, with care and money, the land could be saved and the people restored to it—restored, well, not to prosperity, that was certain, but to a pinch of dignity. Others were convinced that irreversible natural forces were changing the climate of the earth and that this land was forever lost.

News of the drought was played down by the controlled press in Bamako, but there was copious reporting of the cholera epidemic that followed in its wake, probably because members of the government were fearful of its spread. There were thousands of deaths. In one village of 750, five hundred cases of cholera were reported, and three hundred of these victims died—a fatality rate of 60 percent when 10 percent would have been considered "normal" if medical care had been available.

Once the scope of the epidemic was evident, the government moved fast and efficiently. Families, sometimes entire villages, were quarantined. Schools in afflicted villages were closed, and street sales of food were prohibited. Educational campaigns urged people to practice the most rigid standards of sanitation, and soldiers (there was no shortage of these in Mali) went about everywhere pouring chlorine into wells. As a result of this frenetic activity, the epidemic was arrested and people began paying more attention to such simple but essential precautions as the treatment of water and the washing of hands and utensils with soap.

Fanta Falls ill

Just as we were getting used to this disquieting news from the north, illness struck closer to home. Fanta, whom all of us had thought indestructible, fell suddenly and desperately ill, unable to leave her bed except to be led to the latrine. Not cholera, luckily, but one of those parasitical invasions that in Africa take such a toll of the very young and the very old. Aminata moved in with her to do the cooking; Aminata's two preteen daughters Fatamata and Hawa took over my laundry and housekeeping; and twice each day Ami and little Madiné swept the leaves from my courtyard. Emily Furst, the Peace Corps' marvelously compassionate new medical officer and wife of the World Bank's representative in Mali, violated regulations to look at Fanta and to take a stool specimen to the embassy laboratory to be analyzed and then put her through a course of antibiotics. Still Fanta kept getting weaker and weaker. Female relatives and friends from villages as distant as a hundred kilometers flocked to her windowless one-room house. There, they spent the days chatting by Fanta's bedside and performing small, necessary tasks; at night they slept on the floor; all were clearly prepared for the worst.

One afternoon, I was standing by Fanta's bed when she slowly drew her long, bony hand from under the coverlet and feebly grasped my own.

"'M bana, Namory, 'm bana. I am finished, I am finished," she said softly. There was a quick shushing from the older people, and the children began to cry.

"Oh no, Fanta, no!" I responded automatically and gave sleep and I went wordlessly home to eat the rice Aminata had prepared. In the afternoon, while I was teaching, the older relatives took Fanta to the hospital in a taxi.

This strong interdependence of family is, to an American like myself, one of the most seductive features of the Malian culture: We have nothing like it anymore. So long as there remains on earth a single aunt or uncle, grandparent, grandchild, cousin, or second cousin, no Malian is ever permitted to live alone, or to be sick alone, or to die alone.

And yet, in the extreme with which it is practiced here, this family closeness is also a formidable obstacle to democratic development, for it encourages one of the most resistant forms of corruption. Nepotism. A Malian with a good job is not only forgiven for favoring his relatives with appointments and promotions, he is expected to do so and considered disloyal if he doesn't.

At the hospital, the relatives continued their vigil, taking turns bringing Fanta meals of thin gruel, and each night one or more of them would watch by her bedside. None of us was optimistic about her recovery, but evidently Fanta was tougher than she looked. In two weeks she confounded the odds and was out of the hospital, nagging Aminata about her cooking.

9

Partings

A t five-thirty on a clear Monday morning, a few weeks after Fanta's seemingly miraculous recovery, I was abruptly wakened by a loud rapping on my steel window blinds. Two young friends had motor-cycled in from Moribabougou to announce that Balamine Keita, my eighty-seven-year-old adoptive grandfather, the village chief who had hon-ored me with the name of his own father, had died quietly the evening before; his burial was to be in a few hours.

As my *bashèe* pulled into the market square of Moribabougou a little before nine (I was formally dressed in my gold robe, or *grand boubou*, and so could hardly travel by bicycle), it was evident that radio announcements of the old man's death had found their audience: The marketplace was jammed with bat-tered cars and motorcycles and a surprising number of bicycles. I was recog-nized and guided through the crowd to Birama's house and from there to the courtyard of the mosque. After removing my running shoes (the only shoes my feet could wear comfortably), I squatted with the other old men of the vil-lage on one of the woven grass mats laid down for the occasion and waited for the ceremony to begin. All of the women and most of the younger men were gathered elsewhere.

The imam who had introduced me to the mosque during my first summer in Mali (and whom Balamine had termed "famous for his greed") led the crowd, by then numbering into the hundreds, in a few chants and prayers. Balamine's body, barely concealed beneath a faded orange blanket, was carried out of his house on a narrow wooden bed and placed in the center of the courtyard, almost exactly where he and the other old men of the village had gathered to slaughter a young bullock for the feast of Tabaski two years before. There were more prayers and sermons, and a group of elders circulated among the crowd collecting contributions in makeshift cotton bags. Finally, everyone stood up and shook hands with his nearest neighbors, just as some American religionists do at the close of their services. The men closest to the blanket picked up the bamboo bier on which it rested and led the way to the burial site.

It was a curious, cinematic procession—the orange-blanketed body, the robed mourners, the dust hanging in a heavy ochre cloud over the mourners as they straggled purposefully across fields of sun-baked earth and gleaned stalks of millet. I noticed the pallbearers changing shifts more frequently than old Balamine's wasted body should have required, and decided that I, too should lend a hand with the carriage of his body.

There are no coffins in the villages here. At the gravesite, the blanket was removed—to be saved, perhaps, for another occasion—and the approximate shape of Balamine lay visibly on its back, head pointed to the east, feet aimed stiffly upward, hidden only by a shroud of unbleached cotton. Now the wrapped body was lifted from the bier and gently, though not ceremoniously, lowered into the grave. There was no carpet of artificial grass to hide the rough truth of the occasion: The old man was being reunited with the earth. As if to emphasize this, each of the hundreds of mourners pressed forward to cover him, handful by handful, with dampened clay. When came my turn, there was nothing left unburied but the tips of his toes.

Back in the village after the burial, I was ushered with Birama and a score of other elders into the little reception room where Balamine had held court during his final years. I doubt whether more than two or three in the crowd were as old as myself, but most of them looked older. Each took a turn telling stories about the old man. I couldn't understand the stories, of course, because all of them were in the native language, but some must have been quite funny because there was much loud laughter.

The gaiety reminded me of one of the three-sentence reports students were required to present to the debate class during my maiden year at ENSup:

> What I want to say to Mr. Lawder is that, in the society where
> I come from, the death of an old warrior is the occasion for a great

feast. The ancient drums of death must sound, guns and cannons must fire. The ancestral spirits of the clan must appear to accompany the old warrior's soul, and the people must laugh and dance. There will be feasting in Moribabougou for the next three to seven days.

The Last Days

The passing of Balamine made moot the question, if question there was, of my becoming an African farmer. His oldest surviving son was called back to Moribabougou to take over the management of the household. (Birama, though called a "son," was actually a nephew and had no control over the disposition of the property.) This went a long way toward soothing Aisha's fears, and she began talking more confidently about a new life in America.

But a very real problem remained. Living simply in Mali, keeping the same little house and garden, Aisha and I could have just about managed on my social security, with a little extra income from tutoring and freelance writing. To live in the U.S. however, I'd need a real job at decent pay. Could I find one, less than a year from my seventieth birthday?

Aisha, for whatever irrational reasons, was sure of it. Of course, I was old, but I was also wise. And I was healthy and had an intellectual occupation. Accustomed to seeing my lively antics in the classroom, my white hair flying as I biked bravely each day through the streets of the city, she couldn't understand my concerns.

Two months later and a week before leaving for the States to hunt down the job I feared I would never find, I watched Aisha graduate proudly near the top of her class, and that evening, dancing together at the graduation ball, we exposed ourselves for the first time as a couple. It was Aisha's debut on a dance floor and, after a few faltering minutes, she was magnificent.

My final days with old Fanta and her grandchildren were not easy ones. Fanta was misty-eyed and stoic; Madinè clung to me like mistletoe from morning to night; and little Badara refused to admit that Namory was really leaving and flew into a tantrum whenever anyone insisted that I was. Dear, bright, diligent Ami, who had been an unexpected and unearned granddaughter to me ever since I arrived in Bamako, was the hardest of all for me to leave and seemed to have the hardest time with my leaving. For days she hid herself from me and, when she was obliged to come near—to bring my lunch or my laundry—she hid her eyes. In fact, her whole attitude was so uncharacteristically sullen that I came to believe she saw my friendship as having been a betrayal from the start.

90

Mariam and Birama were more stoic, but they were clearly saddened by my departure. Nègue was sure I'd be back. Not because I would fail to find work. Like Aisha, he had a wonderfully unrealistic estimation of the old man's capacities. No, Nègue's belief was based on his unflinching optimism. Aisha would change her mind and consent to live with me in Mali. "Anyway," he said, "you have to come back. This is your country now."

Well, not really. I could never abandon my culture completely. I would always yearn for my children in America and for my extended family there, a family almost as filled with uncles and nieces and nephews and grand-nieces and grand-nephews as any family in Africa. I would always miss the television news. I would always have a yen for a beer or a pork chop and, every few years or so, for a boiled and buttered lobster fresh from the sea. These affections are engraved in my memory, ingrained in my blood.

But I knew by now that I would also be always partly African, whatever the color of my skin. I have an African family—two of them, in fact. At an age when profound friendships are hard to come by, I have made several as viscerally close as any from my youth. And, while Africa has not liberated me entirely from the New England prudishness that has dogged me all of my days, it has indeed helped me to understand myself, and it has opened my mind to new possibilities for living.

There was no room for such philosophic musings in Aisha's mind when she came to see me off at the plane. She was dressed as for a party and her eyes glistened with holiday expectations. Just ahead of us at the airline counter, a group of prosperous-looking Malian businessmen, escorted by their well-nourished wives, were checking in their Gucci bags.

"When we are married," Aisha whispered, "I want to get fat."

El Haji, my landlord

*The road in front of my house
during the rainy season*

Madinè with the twins,
Awa and Adame

One of Balamine's many
children

In my office

With my students

Adame (left) and Awa (below) in America

Book II
(1988-94)
Fishing in the Sky

Time is but the stream I go a-fishing in. I drink at it; but while I drink I see the sandy bottom and detect how shallow it is. Its thin current slides away, but eternity remains. I would drink deeper; fish in the sky, whose bottom is pebbly with stars.

Henry David Thoreau

10

Return of the Prodigal

Nègùèdougou was right. In less than two years I was back in Africa,
living in the same house and once again a Peace Corps volunteer
teaching English at Mali's national teacher's college in Bamako.
"You have to come back," Nègùè had said. "This has become your
country, too."

I didn't return docilely. I had hoped that my three years' experience in
Africa would be an enormous plus in my search for a job teaching English as a
foreign language in America, but to some employers they were just three years
tacked onto my age. I registered with several agencies and managed to get
myself provisionally qualified to teach high-school English in New York City
and in New Jersey, but the school year opened and I was still unemployed.

Mesmerized by my dreams of a life with Aisha, I took a job in Saudi
Arabia, teaching English to Arab cadets at a naval base in Dammam, on the
Persian Gulf. The money was good enough to support a wife, with something
left over, and I expected another interesting adventure, made even more
enjoyable by my easy familiarity with the Muslim culture of Mali. What I was
not prepared for was the closed, sexist structure of Arab society and the way
this made friendly relations with Arab families impossible.

Of course, Mali is a highly sexist society, too. Malian men are the undisputed bosses of their families and Malian women are charged with serving their needs and bearing their children. But within this lopsided framework, most married women, like Mariam and Aminata, have a little freedom. They go to market by themselves. They joke with men. They wear pretty clothes on the street as well as at home. I myself was welcomed into the homes of the most devout believers and invited to join in celebration of the most sacred holidays, and no Malian man thought to hide his wife and daughters from me.

Not so in Saudi Arabia, or in the other fundamentalist states of Arab North Africa. There, men are so persistently conscious of the sexual utility of women that they conceal them from other men behind veils and closed doors and regard the slightest interest in them as aggressive and prurient. One of my colleagues at the naval base was nearly drummed out of class when he tried innocently to encourage conversation by asking a student how many brothers and sisters he had at home.

"What business do you have with my sisters?" the student demanded angrily.

I myself was given lesson plans for teaching the vocabulary of "family life"; they included the English words for "father," "son," "husband," and "brother," but no words for mother, daughter, wife, or sister. No feminine pronouns either.

None of this sexist nonsense seemed to trouble Aisha when I wrote her about it. Instead, her mind was blown by my descriptions of the shops in Dammam City, with their bargain-priced TVs, videos, perfumes, and European fashions, and she saw herself blossoming like Cinderella in a world of plenty she had never imagined within reach. For this miracle, she thought it a small sacrifice to stay hidden indoors all day and go veiled to the market only when her husband or a group of women friends could chaperone her.

My students at the naval base were badly prepared, the syllabus was mechanized, and my uniformed supervisors were arrogant and unforgiving, but I, too, was willing to make sacrifices because I could support Aisha and we could save some money. Before I could send for her, however, the Saudi navy abruptly decided to stop furnishing separate quarters to married teachers. I protested and, not long afterward, an anonymous officer discovered a clause in the Saudi labor code forbidding the employment of foreigners over the age of sixty. I had no decision to make: My uniform was abruptly repossessed and I was returned to America.

Home Again

Peace Corps was more generous and, when I applied for readmission, I was offered a choice of assignments around the globe. The official with whom I spoke seemed astonished when I turned down opportunities in Tahiti, Thailand, and Nepal and opted to return to impoverished, landlocked Mali where I had already spent three years.

This was enough for Aisha. Her letters had become more and more infrequent, and now ceased entirely. A few months after I wrote her to announce my impending return, I received an awkward letter from Nèguèdougou informing me that she had married.

Nèguè assumed I would be heartbroken. Actually, I was relieved. I had long ago accepted the reality that Aisha had higher goals than sharing a three-room cement house with a white-haired American in Bamako, and I was sure she had made the only rational decision—for both of us.

When I arrived in the courtyard of El Haji's warehouse after my two-year absence, Fanta's entire family was lined up waiting for me, each child freshly washed and ironed. Fanta, tough and leathery as ever, took charge of the ritual greetings and asked about the health of every member of my family in America; she hadn't forgotten a name. Madinè, who must now have been almost nine but looked no bigger than before, and her six-year-old brother Badara, who had shot up like a beanstalk and was now almost as tall as his older sister, rushed up and hugged me. Ami, now almost fourteen, was clearly struggling to maintain her dignity, but her wide grin would have done credit to the Cheshire Cat.

Of course everyone noticed immediately the Santa Claus sack I was carrying, so the first order of business had to be the distribution of presents. For Ami and Madinè who had kept me company for over two years at morning coffee and evening study hall, I'd gone overboard, but there were small gifts for everyone—Fanta, Aminata, Badara and his girlish eleven-year-old brother Bua, husky sixteen-year-old Awa, eighteen-year-old Fatoumata who had grown into such spectacular beauty that the whole family was holding its collective breath until she was safely married, and the one already-married daughter, Sali, just back with her taxi-driver husband from four years in Saudi Arabia and nursing her second child. There were even small, pink plastic dolls for Adame and Awa (yes, a second Awa!), twin girls born four months after my departure and now a year and a half old. I had tried vainly to find brown-skinned dolls at dime-store prices, but the little girls seemed just as happy with the pink.

Before the twins were born, Aminata and her husband Aliou had planned to name them "Adama" and "Awa," as Adam and Eve are called in the Qur'an. When Adam and Eve turned out to be a pair of girls, the parents kept the names but feminized "Adama" by dropping the final "a" and changing the pronunciation to a-DAMe. Adame and Awa were as identical as identical twins can be, and all that enabled me to tell them apart at the beginning was a small scar in the center of Awa's forehead where an overenthusiastic mother's helper had dropped her while parading around the neighborhood on a tricycle. It took less than an hour for the twins to decapitate both dolls, but they kept playing with them just the same, ignoring Namory completely and hiding tearfully under their mother's skirt whenever he tried to force an introduction.

Immediately the surprises were passed out, the children rushed into Fanta's one-room house to try on their Sears and Roebuck finery, and when Ami returned in her new American frock, she brought with her the plastic chess set I had left behind. She then proudly demonstrated that she remembered exactly how to set up the pieces on the board and shyly suggested that we interrupt the festivities with a game. Madinè watched us play as if she understood what she was doing, but after a few minutes went back into the house to fill her new red knapsack (monogrammed with a big yellow M for McDonald's) with old schoolbooks; she wore the sack on her back for the rest of the afternoon.

Aminata, the mother of these seven girls and two boys, was not yet forty and seemed not to have aged at all during my two years away. Once the children had carefully folded away their new clothes, she served up a big bowl of rice and tomato-onion sauce, with a tiny bit of meat that was pointedly reserved for the guest of honor. Little Ami had done the cooking.

Fanta told me that El Haji was unhappy with the motorcycle repair business that had taken over my old house next door; the lessees had torn down a couple of interior walls without his permission and had turned the garden into a driveway and dumping ground for discarded parts. Worse, they were behind in their rent. Fanta was sure she could persuade El Haji to kick them out and give the house back to me. I asked her to try.

She also told me at length and with emotion what an unworthy fiancée I had left behind. "After you were gone," she complained, "Aisha came here only once to bring me news of you, but Nèguèdougou came many times. Aisha is not good for you, Namory. She only wants your money."

Within a week of my return, as if in celebration, the skies opened wide over Bamako and poured rain down long and hard nearly every day, sometimes twice. Mud was inches deep in most of the streets and potholes were almost impossible to detect before dropping into them. In front of my old house next to Fanta's, the road was utterly impassable for vehicles, and the only way pedestrians could get in and out was via the narrow roman road I had built for my bicycle four years earlier. The courtyard itself was flooded right up to the doorsills of the house, and I hoped Fanta wouldn't succeed in her mission to El Haji until the rainy season was over. This was the best rainy season Mali had enjoyed for years, and I kept telling myself that what was good for the country was good for Namory Keita, but it was an effort.

In Moribabougou, the farming village where I had begun my stay in Mali, the heavy rains had turned the village into a replica of Berlin at the close of the war. Mud walls had tumbled down or simply dissolved, so that each separate household now merged into the next. In many cases, latrine walls had disappeared entirely and been replaced by bundles of small branches or by sheets of tin roofing. A few of the older houses had just melted away.

However, this was a village of farmers, and the complications that the heavy rains had brought were more than offset by the promise of a good harvest, so no one had much trouble.

Nor did I have time for such reflections when I arrived in the village for still another feast of Tabaski. I had just turned my bike off the main road when I heard a huge shout in a vaguely familiar feminine voice. The youthful face from which the cry emanated seemed also familiar, but this face was attached to a most unfamiliarly curvaceous body. I was still struggling for memory when, without warning, this delicious-looking, half-known creature threw itself into my arms and kissed me smack on the lips and right in the middle of the street!

"Welcome back, Don!" the voice exclaimed in heavily accented but quite recognizable English.

This nubile young lady, I was quickly reminded, was my cousin Fatoumata Keita, the same young girl who had greeted me outside Mariam and Birama's house on my first evening in Moribabougou five years ago, and who had then announced that she was going to study English at a lycée in Bamako so she could return with me to the U.S. Now she had indeed finished the lycée and passed her two baccalaureate exams—an almost unheardof feat for an obscure farmer's daughter from a poor village in the country—and in October she was scheduled to matriculate in the department of history/geography at ENsup.

As we walked hand in hand to my family's house, I noticed that Tata, as she liked to be called, walked with a conspicuous limp; one of her legs was a bit shorter than the other, a residue of the infantile paralysis that takes such a toll among children here. Tata took me on a house tour of the Keita clan so I could shake hands with all the children and pass out cola nuts to their elders. No one seemed surprised to see me back, but the village seemed empty without Balamine.

Tata was present during all this, often serving as my semi-official translator. The evening before, Mariam had called me aside to say I should be wary of her. "She is like Aisha," she said. "All she wants is your money." Poor Aisha!

Her failure to keep in touch with my families, Fanta included, during the two years I was gone did not help her reputation.

In spite of Mariam's warning, which I took seriously, I let myself enjoy my time with Tata. Her dress and manner had become so thoroughly influenced by American films and rock-and-roll performers that I told her she was becoming a *farafin tubabou*, a black European. She took this as a compliment and told me it was her ambition to get a college degree and then "a very high position in the government." She said this would "bring pride to the whole village," but I suspected there was something of the vengeful "I'll show them all!" attitude in her motivation.

In any case, I was convinced that Tata would get what she wanted, or something close to it, even though she hadn't a political connection in the world. She was both gutsy and ambitious and had already lifted herself to an extraordinary height for a gimpy-legged girl from a poor and almost illiterate family. Tata had ideas about using me, of course, and these I found entirely logical; I only wished I were in a more influential position to be used.

Wherever I went in Bamako, I was surprised by enthusiastic cries of recognition from townspeople I didn't remember at all and from former students whose faces I for the most part remembered but whose names I had thoroughly forgotten, and soon word of my return seemed everywhere. "Namory! Namory!" I was greeted, and "How are you, old man?" I had grossly underestimated the retentive power of an old man's image, white hair flying as he whirred through the thronged streets of Bamako on his bicycle.

Bamako had grown enormously, and at both ends of the economic spectrum. There were more foreigners here than ever, almost all of them attached to one or another of the international aid organizations that had set up headquarters in Mali (Peace Corps itself had almost trebled in size). Everywhere there had sprouted small "supermarkets" and cafes catering to European tastes.

There had also been a noticeable influx of migrants from the villages and dry areas bordering the desert. The most conspicuous sign of their displacement was the presence downtown of a new class of beggars—children of the once proud town of a new class of beggars—children of the once proud Tuareg nomads of the Sahara. These handsome people, whose women are discreetly veiled and whose turbaned men look like arrogant replicas of Rudolf Valentine in *The Sheik*, have never considered themselves bound by the laws of any government, not the colonial regime of the French, and especially not the black rulers of independent Mali. Now, the advancing desert was scattering them all over West Africa.

As I strode through Bamako's crowded market, I would feel a forefinger suddenly grasped by a tiny hand tugging for attention. I would look down and see two enormous black eyes set in a tiny, small-featured, and very light-skinned face, the prototype of those horribly sentimental "original oil paintings" featured in the windows of cheap framing shops all over the world. My first response was a predictably sympathetic one, but this was quickly overtaken by a kind of quiet anger as I looked down the street to see the appealing child's demoralized mama or papa squatting inconspicuously in a corner, waiting for the loot. I saw many such children in Bamako now, or perhaps the same ones kept reappearing, for I was accosted like this several times in each block, my fingers grasped by little hands in the same pathetic way.

I looked for Hawa, the leper woman, in front of the national bank where I was used to seeing her squatting with her begging bowl, but the bank had gone bankrupt and Hawa and all the other beggars and petty traders who had held forth there had disappeared. I never saw Hawa again.

L'École Normale Supérieure, when I returned to teach English after an absence of two years, was an entirely different place. It looked the same. There were the same broken desks and chairs, the same worn-out blackboards on which nothing legible could be written, and in only a handful of classrooms was there working electricity for lights and ceiling fans. But, except for myself and a personable and experienced teacher named Sally Olsonofsky who joined the faculty a few months later, there wasn't a single white face in the English department where there had been nine or ten before.

Some of these American Peace Corps volunteers had been very good indeed and were sorely missed, but the total number was large enough to constitute its own society, so there was always a clear, if friendly division in the faculty—Malians and non-Malians. Not racist, really, but almost. However, while I was away Peace Corps had shifted its emphasis from teacher training to primary education, and the Ministry of Education had been obliged to replace them with Malians promoted from the lycées. Like most Malian teachers of English, they were strong in grammar and weak in literature.

All in all, though, the change seemed to have been a healthy one, for there was now a conspicuous sense of team spirit in the department. This new camaraderie may also have been partly due to the department's effervescent new chairman, Mamadou Gueye, who had replaced his friend Ousmane Minta who had become, as he himself confessed, "completely burnt out" by bureaucratic pressures. Sharp-tongued, razor-thin Souleyman Ba, who had once tried to teach me how to persuade female students to exchange kisses for passing grades, had been demoted to assistant: His credentials were discovered to be phony and he didn't even have a master's degree, let alone the Ph.D. he had claimed. He probably should have been fired, but Gueye felt sorry for him and, anyway, he needed one more warm body on the staff.

105

Souleyman was assigned to teach British civilization, which nobody else in the department, himself included, knew very much about and for which there were no textbooks whatever.

With only one other native-speaker in the department, I had pretty much my pick of courses. I kept nineteenth century American studies (civilization and literature) and my third-year composition course, but was induced by Gueye to take on first-year phonetics; he promised me that I could teach students the pronunciation of English by exercises in speech without over-reliance on the technical side of phonetics, which I had studied for only one semester at Brooklyn College twenty-five years before.

Fanta was as good as her word and, five months after my receded, she persuaded El Haji to evict the motorcycle repair shop and rent the house to me once again. It was shabbier than ever, with broken light switches, a toilet that refused to flush on cue, and a garden that had sadly deteriorated under the care, or lack thereof, of the philistines who had occupied the place during my absence. I fixed the switches and the toilet and ordered a truckload of coarse sand and two wagonsful of horse manure for the garden. Ami, Madinè, and I spent two days digging these last into the hard, impoverished soil, and Fanta began once again bringing me green sticks to plant. I did not know it, but the garden we made that week was a commitment to permanence.

Before leaving Bamako, I had had the lucky foresight to leave my rickety, unsalable bamboo furniture with the Peace Corps for any new volunteers who wanted it. When the children discovered it was still there, filthy with dust but otherwise intact, they were in seventh paradise, to coin a Muslim term. They remembered where every piece had been placed nearly three years before and insisted that this was the only way to arrange things now. Ami, now almost fourteen, was most unhappy to discover that the computer chess machine against which she used to struggle so valiantly (and once in a while successfully) was not among the articles recovered; I had left it back in the U.S. and was now obliged to send for it.

It was like old times. Each evening at around eight o'clock. Ami and Madinè would bring over their schoolbooks for a couple of hours of study by electric light. Most of their lessons were in Arabic, and many required them to memorize passages from the Qur'an, so the living room was abuzz each evening with the soft hum of Islamic prayers.

There were ghosts, of course. One evening when I was arranging my bookcase, out tumbled an envelope addressed to me in Aisha's hand. It had never been mailed but had apparently been mixed with the books and other documents I had left behind with her because of the high air-freight costs. The plan had been for her to take the sack to Peace Corps and arrange for it to be shipped by the slower, but far cheaper, surface mail. She did her part, but for other, irrelevant reasons the sack never did get shipped and was waiting for me in the Peace Corps office when I returned. The envelope had lain unnoticed in the sack until I moved back into my old house two years later.

In the envelope was a letter dated August 23, 1986, six weeks after my departure, placed where I might find it later. Aisha apologized for not delivering the books to Peace Corps promptly, as promised, but she had kept the sack in her room because, "Every time I see this bag I think that DON has not gone yet. Today, I unwillingly decide to bring it to Peace Corps because it should be sent to you. I consider today as the date of your departure."

There came uninvited to my mind a short poem by Robert Frost—only eight lines long—which I had introduced to my class the tour before.

> Nature's first green is gold,
> Her hardest hue to hold.
> Her early leaf's a flower;
> But only so an hour.
> Then leaf subsides to leaf.
> So Eden sank to grief,
> So dawn goes down to day.
> Nothing gold can stay.

My relationship with Aisha had seemed a kind of gold for both of us and we had not been able to hold it. I think what happened—to each of us at pretty much the same time—was that we became discouraged. Nothing lasts forever, gold or otherwise, and we had waited hopefully for just too long. All relationships are bargains. I wanted to live with her in Africa; she insisted I demonstrate my love by carrying her off to America first. Reasonable, honest, both of us, and for a while pure gold. But the issues were unnegotiable, and the waiting went on too long.

11

Will I Ever Get to Timbuktoo?

I had never forgotten my dream of climaxing my African stay with a scenic trip downriver to Timbuktoo and, during my second year back in Bamako, I made up my mind definitely to go. However, the unseasonably light summer rains had made steamboat travel once again impossible and I was obliged to choose between making the tedious journey overland by car and truck, or not making it at all. Predictably I turned to Nèguèdougou for help, and at three o'clock on a Thursday afternoon, at the beginning of spring vacation, I made my way to a stall in the market where he had reserved a place for me on a trailer truck headed for "the mysterious city." I advanced five thousand francs as down payment for a place in the truck's cab with the driver and two other travelers. I could have saved money by riding in back on top of the cargo with the forty-odd other passengers, but it was a two-day trip and I opted for luxury.

At seven o'clock, Salif Maiga, the Songhai merchant who had organized the safari, explained that he still needed more cargo to justify the trip and invited me to share his bowl of rice while we waited. At nine o'clock he gave up hope, and I was transferred to a back seat in a Land Rover headed for the town of Dirè; from there, I was to find my own transportation for the remaining ninety kilometers to the mysterious city.

I had thought, after my earlier travels in the bush, that I was tough and could handle everything, but I was wrong. The first three hours were not too bad. There were only eight of us in back, four to a side on facing seats, the only real awkwardness being the spare tires on the floor between us. After we passed the police checkpoint in Segou, however, the driver saw a chance to make a few extra francs for himself and packed in an additional nine people and their baggage—two extra on each side bench, two more in front, and three on the spare tires in back, which, until now, had been our only legroom.

I shan't try your patience with an account of my discomfort during the next hours, just confess that there were moments when I would have betrayed my mother for room to wiggle my toes or to shift my hips half an inch one way or the other. My knees, of course, were the first part of my anatomy to go; when we paused for a rest stop, I could scarcely stagger to the side of the road. (The word "weak-kneed" must have been coined in a situation like this.) We kept going through the sleepless night until, at around 4 A.M., the driver pulled off the road in the market town of Niono so he himself could doze off for an hour or two.

At six, we started up again, but the load we were carrying now proved even harder on the car than on the passengers, and just as the sun reached an angle of about sixty degrees overhead, the right rear spring snapped. Grateful to be out of our seats in any case, we found shelter under a couple of scraggly thorn trees while the driver took the car back to Niono for repairs; he took with him three of the latest arriving passengers who would have to wait for better luck. We got going again a little after noon, crawling on the corduroy road at about twenty to twenty-five miles per hour to ease the strain on the jury-rigged rear spring. After every large bump, our driver would halt the car, clamber out, and check the undercarriage. Squeezed like an old lemon in my airless seat, massaging my wasted knees, I thought of the far more painful journey of the Joad family westward to California, but I was not comforted.

Interesting country. I wish I had been in a better mood to appreciate it. The area around Niono is extensively irrigated by a series of canals radiating from the Niger river, and there are green fields of rice and millet everywhere. After about 100 kilometers, though, the irrigated area ends, and the real Sahel begins. The word "sahel" is from the Arabic, meaning "shore," and really the landscape is like that of the seashore except that a desert has replaced the water. Sand stretches in all directions to the horizon, broken only by occasional scrub trees and thorny bushes. Here and there we passed small herds of animals, mostly sheep and goats but some cattle as well, tended by Fulani shepherds wearing their traditional conical hats as protection from the dazzling sun. Occasionally we passed children leading donkeys laden with firewood, and once a small group of camels. Two or three times during the afternoon, we passed small Fulani villages with their distinctive, dome-shaped huts of grass.

At about four in the afternoon, as this old man was approaching his limit of exhaustion, we limped into the village of Nampala, about thirty-five kilometers from the Mauretanian border. As we shook out our near-paralyzed bones, the driver confessed that, because of our crippled progress, we'd have to spend one more night in the car before reaching Dirè. At that awful moment, a group of young Americans emerged from a nearby mud house and, noticing a fellow American, identified themselves as archeologists on a dig into African history. There would be plenty of other rides available tomorrow, they said, so why not spend the night in the village with them? My grateful knees answered before my lips. In the following days, no one came by who would carry me to Timbuktoo, and so began a serendipitous week excavating history and prehistory in this remote pocket of civilization.

A Frontier Skirmish

There were five members of the archeological team—three graduate students from Rice University (one of these a Malian) working on their Ph.D.'s, and two oversized Canadian women taking time out from school to help. Since the country here is far too dry for mosquitoes, we slept outdoors on woven grass mats spread on the sand. Each morning at about seven-thirty, I would help my hosts load their four-wheel-drive car and truck with buckets and tools and watch them take off with eight or ten Fulani workmen for the two separate sites they were exploring. Each evening, I helped them unload. They must have been starved for company, for they treated me royally, buying me Coca-Colas, filling my plate first at dinner, making me instant cocoa at bedtime, reserving for me always one of the two folding chairs they had in camp. They kept urging me to join them, but I was determined to get on to Timbuktoo, and for the first few days I stayed close to the village, hoping to cadge a ride.

Nampala is not really a village, but an *arondissement*, a kind of township made up of about twenty scattered settlements, the largest of which houses the commandant, an infirmary, a dilapidated four-room schoolhouse, a small mosque, and an outdoor truck stop where travelers can buy fried cakes, lukewarm sodas, and meals of rice and goat meat. There are about twenty-five mud houses in Nampala proper, and a slightly larger number of domed grass huts in the Fulani village alongside. In the center of all this is a great mound that houses Nampala's water supply, a well that has been dug down more than fifty meters to reach the declining water table. The water is brought up by donkey power. The beasts are hitched one at a time to windlasses and, as they walk lazily downhill, they draw the water up into small cement troughs for the sheep, goats, and cattle and into separate small reservoirs for the humans. Anyone who does not have a donkey (or a couple of husky wives) for pulling must buy his water at 100 francs a bucket. Morning and evening, the well site is thronged like a DeMille spectacular with turbaned shepherds and their thirsty flocks and herds. During the heat of the day, while the animals are off grazing and browsing in the bush, the area is quiet and deserted.

But this pastoral scene, with its echoes of Abraham and Moses, was deceptive. Just twenty five miles northeast of Nampala is the border of the Moorish nation of Mauretania, whose white-skinned seminomads are perhaps even poorer than their black-skinned brothers in Mali, and certainly more warlike. The morning after my arrival, a wounded Malian frontier guard staggered into the village with news of a furious night attack on his lonely outpost by truck-loads of Moorish raiders armed with AK-47s. The fact that he had incurred his wounds by fleeing blindly into a thornbush in the middle of the night might have injured the credibility of his story if he had not been followed a few hours later by an army command car.

I have since learned that armed conflict has for years been a fact of life in the areas bordering the desert. The white-skinned Moors, like their ethnic cousins, the nomadic Tuaregs of the Sahara, are fiercely proud of their bandit history and have never accepted the equality of their sedentary black neighbors to the south; even today there are pockets within Mauretania where slavery is practiced, even though forbidden by law.

A Visit to a Country School

While hanging about waiting for the ride that never came, I took time to sit in on a few classes at the primary school just beyond the well. What a terribly difficult job these bush teachers have! Classes for grades one through six were held in two mud-brick buildings, which had been so ravaged by the last year's rains that only three classrooms were useable. But then there were only three teachers for the six grades, so the classes would have had to be doubled up anyway. First grade met with second, third with fourth, and fifth with sixth. As a fellow teacher from Bamako, I was made graciously welcome.

My first visit was to the classroom shared by the sixth grade (three boys and two girls) and the fifth (six boys and five girls (I'm told that this attrition rate was typical). The official starting hour for school was 7:30, but the class didn't get underway until after 8:00. The teacher explained that most of the students live far from the school, some as distant as six to seven kilometers, and that is why they were always late. Reading came first, and both fifth and sixth graders took turns reading aloud a short passage entitled "Un Accident d'Automobile." The teacher asked questions to test their comprehension, and the students answered by finding the appropriate sentences in the text and reading them aloud word for word.

After reading came arithmetic, and again the two grades worked together on the same problem—a rather tricky one, I thought, involving the monthly payments over a six-month period for a triangular field priced at so much per square meter. While the children were struggling with this, I moved over to the first and second grade classroom. Here, of course, there was no way of teaching the two groups at the same time, for the second graders were reading words and simple phrases, while the first graders were still trying to recognize and pronounce letters and syllables. The older group waited its turn in amazingly good order while the younger children worked with the teacher.

What ferocious eagerness these little ones showed! They were learning to read and write syllables beginning with the letter *b*. The teacher would write an example on the board and the students would copy it with chalk on their slates. Almost as soon as the example was given, the room would echo with shrill, competing cries of *"moi!" "moi!"* Students in the back rows left their seats and moved to the front for attention. Then those left behind leapfrogged to the front of these, and so on uncontrollably until the hapless teacher, wife of the area commandant, was literally under siege. Twenty minutes of this and the process was repeated with the vowel combination *ou* and, when the break came at 10:00, everyone was ready for it.

The recess was supposed to last fifteen minutes, but none of the teachers seemed in a hurry to call the students back to class, so school didn't resume until eleven, a full hour later. About twenty minutes into class, word was received that a truck carrying fresh mangoes had just arrived from Niono, and all three teachers bolted from their classrooms to buy the fresh fruit.

The next two mornings I watched more of the same, and was again struck by the contrast between the eagerness of the children and the lethargy of the teachers. It was hard to fault the latter—underpaid, underappreciated, marooned at the edge of a watering hole for sheep and goats and a good two hours from a town where they could find fresh fruits or vegetables or maybe see a movie. Still, the handful of children who had been encouraged by their parents to seek an education (enrollment is less than 3 percent of those eligible) were clearly not getting what they craved.

During a break on one of the following mornings, students of the fifth and sixth grades were invited to choose books from the tiny library donated by a village in France that had decided to adopt Nampala as a sister community.

The youngsters crowded like Christmas shoppers around the table where the books were kept, and each child was allowed to borrow one book. Some took stories to read, but most went for textbooks on math and history. They could take the books home and keep them for one week.

Digging up the Past

Late Monday morning, three days after my arrival in Nampala, I came to the conclusion that, even if transport to Timbuktoo did arrive, I could never get there and back to Bamako in time for my classes. Anyway, I reasoned, I was letting my preconceived notions take charge of my life when my original purpose had been simply to record and respond to life as it actually happened. I had stumbled across another small adventure to be lived, and I was letting my prearranged plans keep me from it.

My new friends were working in two teams, each team tackling a different site about an hour's driving apart. On my first day, Helen took me in charge. Together with the Malian archeologist Tereba Togola and a couple of diggers hired locally, we headed for the youngest of the two sites, a huge mound covering the ruins of Iron-Age settlements dating from about 800 to 1500. This would have been roughly the period beginning with the earliest Muslim incursions into sub-Saharan Africa and continuing through the rise and fall of the great Keita kings of Timbuktoo and the Empires of Ghana and Mali.

Our four-wheel-drive pickup truck took us comfortably across the wide plain of sand and scrub that surrounded the mound in every direction. Along the way we passed a few ragged Fulani herdsmen tending their small holdings of sheep and goats, but apart from these and plentiful signs of termites, jackals, and kangaroo rats near the site itself, I saw no other signs of living creatures.

Once on the scene though, it was impossible to miss the evidence of early human habitation. The mound, which rises from the surrounding flatness like the beginnings of a huge pimple, is littered with potsherds, fragments of old clay pots once buried by the windblown sand and then washed to the surface by centuries of summer rains. Most of these fragments are small, but some are nearly whole and many of the larger pieces bear geometric designs that time has hardly obscured. These isolated finds were of no more than passing interest to my archeologist friends, however; they were looking for walls, hearths, animal bones, pottery in context—clues that might explain who those earlier people were, where they came from, what they ate, and how they lived.

In the months before my arrival, my new friends had dug a neat, square hole about two meters deep and a meter and a half on each side, through a dozen centuries of habitation. They had searched and sifted each cubic centimeter of clay and loam, sorted and bagged every artifact, and mapped their locations. From these, they surmised that they were now unearthing traces of West African life at some time early in the second millennium A.D., perhaps around the year 1200, and they knew from the prevalence of fish bones in the debris that this arid place was then surrounded by water.

Their first finds, though historically meaningful, were mostly routine. Then yesterday (my arrival brought them luck, Helen said), they uncovered something special—the bejeweled skeleton of a young woman. Her hair had been braided and decorated with cowrie shells, the principal trading currency of her time and more valuable than gold; a necklace of carnelian lay in ruins about her neck; and heavy copper bracelets still encircled the bones of her wrists. Her teeth showed she had been of child-bearing age, somewhat older than seventeen and younger than thirty-five, and perhaps, Helen guessed, giving birth is how she died. The eastward orientation of the head suggested she had been Muslim, but the ornaments were certainly pagan.

None of the jewelry was of local origin, so this isolated mound, now six hours' journey by car from the nearest crossroads, must once have been on a caravan route, or else within shopping reach of some vanished medieval market town. Possibly, the wealthy young woman buried here had come herself from some farther place. Quite likely, her family paid tribute to one of the early emperors of Mali or Gao, and, almost certainly, she knew of the great Islamic library and university that had just been founded some kilometers to the north, at Timbuktoo.

Tereba Togola, the Malian archeologist in the group, took over my site visits after the first day. Now I was no longer allowed to hoist heavy pails of clay nor to clamber down the carved clay steps to the bottom of the excavations. Instead, I was encouraged to rake through the already sifted debris in the forlorn hope of finding some artifact more professional eyes had missed. Water was pressed on me at every opportunity, and soon the excitement of adventure was gone. I was being treated with full traditional respect as an old man.

The youngest of the archaeologists was a whiz kid named Kevin McDonald, whose undergraduate thesis about coaxing meaning from bones got him a fellowship at Cambridge University where he would work for his Ph.D. when this project was over.

Kevin was fond of making deliberately inane remarks and punctuating them with irritating giggles. As soon as I met him, I knew he was a reincarnation of Albert Campion, Margery Allingham's brilliant but profoundly supercilious detective. I happened to be carrying her book *Mystery Mile* with me, and I gave it to Kevin to read; he was delighted with the comparison.

Kevin was working some kilometers from the others, at a Neolithic, or late Stone Age, site. He was trying to trace the history of the settlement from the nature of the bones left behind. For how many millennia had men lived there? Had they lived there continuously or had they abandoned the site from time to time and then returned? If the latter, what catastrophe caused them to leave? And why did their descendants come back to the same place generations later?

I had told the group I wrote poetry and was planning a book in prose about my journey to Timbuktoo. One final evening under the stars, they asked me to read to them. One poem, "The Wild Bird," they liked especially and made me read it a second time:

> Woe
> to him who has found the wild bird
> and has no searching more.
>
> Sorrow
> to her who has filled the inn:
> the child waits at the door.
>
> Beware
> the full cup.
>
> Foreswear
> the final word.
>
> Keep ever
> an empty room in the inn.
>
> Find never
> the wild bird.

Helen commented, "Maybe the idea of your book should be that Timbuktoo is like the wild bird—a place you never get to."

The trip back was sheer luxury. My archeologist friends were returning to Bamako to ship their trophies to Houston for laboratory analysis and insisted I delay my departure a couple of days so I could ride with them. I sat with my legs stretched out in the spacious front seat of their Land Rover. Tereba drove. I chatted, watched the scenery, munched sandwiches, and alternately dozed

115

off. Twelve painless hours later I was back in my house being greeted by four sleepy children.

The children waited until morning to tell me that, two days after I had left, my "father" Birama Keita, who had welcomed me into his home when I first arrived in Mali, had died painlessly in his sleep. Mariam had no record of his age, but I supposed he was in his early sixties.

I had returned too late to attend Birama's burial, which in hot countries like Mali always takes place the day after death, but I rode out to Moribabougou two days later to pay my respects to Mariam. Following custom, she was in seclusion, permitted to receive visits only from women and close family; she was allowed out only for necessary trips to the latrine and was then accompanied always by another woman. I was family, though, and invited to sit for hours with her in the hot and stuffy little room she had shared with Birama. She was obviously lonely in her forced isolation and had a great need to talk. I understood nothing, but she took my periodic nods and grunts as tokens of serious interest and kept on talking.

I was grateful when Birama's younger brother, little Mamadou Ba, interrupted to suggest I might want to visit his brother's gravesite. The freshly covered mound was in an area of cleared brush next to Balamine's, but there was a difference. Muslim tradition forbids the decoration of graves, even their marking with the names of the deceased, but at the head of Birama's burial mound was a small slab of painted wood, crudely lettered with the one word, "Birama." This was the only grave so marked, and Mamadou Ba turned his eyes away when I looked at him questioningly.

12

Playing Grandfather

With Aisha out of the picture and a productive life in America now seemingly out of reach, I shifted the focus of my attention to my African grandchildren. I call them my grandchildren because that's what my Malian neighbors call them, Namori ka modew—"Namory's grandchildren." Except for the youngest, we have now shared our lives with varying degrees of intimacy for over a dozen years.

But after these many years together, how can I describe them without making them seem too ordinary, too much like American children of the same age? Because they are *different*—different in the ways all children are different from one another, but also different in special ways because they are African.

First of all, African children are, with rare and pathological exceptions, unswervingly respectful to their elders, even to their elder siblings. They eat separately from their fathers and older brothers, dipping their right hands into the bowl they share with their mother and sisters. And all of them, the girls especially, work when American children would be playing.

In the country, both boys and girls help out in the fields and are too often kept out of school for the purpose. Here in the city, they bring wood to the fire, wash clothes, and sweep the yard and the street in front; as soon as they

117

are old enough to count change, they are entrusted with the family's small errands. This year, nine-year-old Madinè goes every morning to the bakery to buy our morning bread. Three years ago, it was Ami. Next year, it will be Badara. And they do all this cheerfully, even joyfully. It seems to me that there is no clear line between what is work and what is play.

And I have another problem. Even as I described them, they were changing, just as all children change, just as Africa itself is changing—from one year to the next, from one month to the next, even from day to day, though this is often difficult to see. Here I will introduce them as I found them during the first months after my return to Bamako.

The Schoolgirls—Ami and Madinè

Two of my grandchildren, Ami and Madinè, you have already met. The latter, no matter how often I told myself how different Malian children are from American children, reminded me inescapably of my older daughter Linda when she was the same age. Madinè was a little actress—so bright, so graceful, so quick! Too quick, in fact, for her own good. Like Linda, she insisted on doing everything right away, without troubling to learn how. When she helped her grandmother Fanta with the cooking, she would take over, spill things, add too much salt, knock pots into the fire, and so she was always getting slapped or scolded. I worried that she might be having the same kinds of problems in the fourth grade at school. Fortunately, the culture here, for all its rigidities, is much more patient with children, more supportive of their needs to grow. Besides, Madinè was blessed with an adoring older sister, Ami, who watched over her like a second mother.

Ami was the kind of fourteen-year-old daughter that parents everywhere must dream of having. If my sons weren't already so well-married, I would want to stash her away so one of them could marry her when she's grown old enough. Where Madinè's intelligence was sparkling and quick, Ami's was deep, like the gleam in a ruby. At eight she had taught herself to play chess by watching me make the moves; at ten she would play for hours at a time against my computer, seldom winning but always hanging in. At her Franco-Arabic school, she was always first or second in her class, and already one of her great concerns was how to clamber back onto the main educational track when her Qur'anic education was done.

By American standards. Ami has had a hard life. She was three years old when she came with her older sister Awa to keep their grandmother Fanta company in her room in El Haji's warehouse. When Ami became old enough to shop, cook, and wash clothes, Awa went back to her mother's and Ami stayed on. Daytimes during the school year, Fanta used to look after herself

118

but, now that she's become more feeble, Aminata and her eldest daughter Fatamata have chipped in for Aminata and her eldest daughter Fatamata have chipped in for a part-time servant girl who is poorer than any of them. When school is out at three, the servant girl leaves and Ami takes over again. She cooks and launders until time to bathe her two-year-old sisters and take the pair of them back to their other's for the night.

Grandmother Fanta is tough and demanding and she runs her tiny household in the traditional autocratic way. However, she knows what school means to Ami and she releases her for a couple of hours each evening to make salad for Namory and Madinè and to study under Namory's electric lights.

Ami is fastidious. She washes her hands each time before and after she touches a plate or a utensil or a piece of bread. Each evening when she prepares our staple salad, she peels the tomatoes and washes each leaf of lettuce separately. And when she serves the salad Malian-style in a common bowl, she gives each person a fork though she has never eaten except with her right hand. Once, I cooked up spaghetti and showed the girls how to eat it Italian-style, using a tablespoon to twirl it neatly onto a fork. She will now eat spaghetti in no other way.

Madinè, when she tried to copy Ami, would invariably overdo. She would carve the tomatoes into too-tiny pieces, then plunge them and the chopped onion and the peeled slices of cucumber into a bowl of water where she would swish them around until they were saturated; then she would forget to drain them.

I never saw Ami play as other children do. She laughed, she joked, she seemed to be having a good time even when she was working but, except for her chess, she never played. When she wasn't working or at school or with me, she was always with Fanta and Fanta's women friends, gabbing away like one of them. Madinè, on the other hand, was always playing. Friends would stop by in the morning to walk with her to school and return in the afternoon to play hopscotch or a kind of jump rope in the street.

The Schoolboys—Bua and Badara

Raised in a household with seven sisters, twelve-year-old Bua seems almost too sweet and gentle to be a boy. He cooks, sews, and helps around the house; he can even iron his sisters' clothes. Still, I doubt Bua is confused about his sexuality, for he likes rough games and spends hours playing soccer (called "football" here) in the street with other boys from the neighborhood. He has also built a small reputation in the family as someone who can fix anything— watches, toys, radios, whatever. When the mechanism in my toilet broke

119

down and refused to flush, Bua was immediately summoned by his mother and quickly put it right, though I think he had never seen a flush toilet before.

Bua needs help, though. He's just getting by in school where, his mother told me, he is regarded as a "playboy," and when he comes over on Sunday mornings to join Ami and Madinè for breakfast, it's painfully obvious that he can't understand French even as well as Madinè, who is two grades behind him; we've stopped trying to interest him in our weekly English lessons.

This is five-year-old Badara's first year in the *jardin des enfants*, or kindergarten, and if he were a girl, he would wear a little curl right in the middle of his forehead. Most of the time Badara is very, very good, flashing a big, gap-toothed grin that makes me want to snatch him up like a Raggedy Andy doll and hug him, but when he is bad, he is horrid. This happens mostly when he is fighting with Madinè. My students tell me that sibling rivalry is a heavy problem in polygamous families, but in the monogamous families I've come to know, like this one, brothers and sisters get on remarkably well. Perhaps this is because of the clear-cut roles assigned to males and females, young and old, from the very beginning of their lives, or perhaps it arises from the socialized way in which Malian children are brought up, but I've seldom seen brothers and sisters fighting, no matter how close in age. Mostly, they are touchingly supportive of one another.

Not so Badara and Madinè. They will seem to be getting along famously for hours. Then one of them will take or want something from the other, Madinè will scream to Fanta for help, Badara will haul off and paste her, Madinè will paste him back, and they will both fall shrieking and wrestling to the ground. Or maybe it will be Madinè who lands the first punch; I can never tell who is responsible.

One day while I was taking lunch at Fanta's, I finally got so fed up with their shouting and screaming that I picked Madinè up, bent her over my knee, and spanked her until she cried real tears. Then, not knowing who was to blame, I pulled Badara out of hiding and spanked him. This was harder, because little Badara was determined to be as tough as a Dead End Kid from the Lower East Side. He refused to show the slightest sign of pain, just grinned infuriatingly. Finally, when I realized that he would never give up even if I went on beating him forever, I stopped. He gave me a weak and crooked grin, intended to show triumph, and limped off before the tears could fall.

While I was punishing the children, the rest of the family made no move to intervene, and Fanta was vociferous in her approval. "Good, Namory, good! Those children are bad! They deserve to be beaten!"

Corporal punishment is the norm here. Usually it is done with a stick or a leafy branch, seldom with the hands. Parents beat their children, teachers beat their pupils, and, rather more often than one might expect, husbands beat their wives. It is as though they don't know any other way to make the others obey. I rather think that Badara and Madinè just didn't understand that I meant business with my scoldings. The spanking they did understand and, while nothing would stop their perpetual bickering, they have never again taken fists to each other in my presence. Nor have I ever spanked them again, or any child.

My punishment of the children had an important side effect. Here, the education of children is a community responsibility, and every older person is supposed to take part in it. If an adult sees a child behaving badly in the absence of the parcorrection, without waiting for permission. My actions marked a new stage in my relationships. From this time on, I was a member of the community.

The Twins—Adame and Awa

Forty years ago, when I was editing *The Menninger Quarterly* in Topeka, Kansas, the Director of Research at the Menninger Foundation was a psychologist named Sibylle Escalona. Billy, as everyone called her, was especially interested in the study of infants and later published some highly regarded work on the development of twins. How she would have envied me my observation post here in Bamako! Three months after my departure to America and almost two years before my return to Bamako, Aminata had given birth to her eighth and ninth children, identical twin girls named Adame and Awa, or "Adam" and "Eve." Every morning at about seven o'clock, the little girls would arrive at my house, swaddled on the backs of Aminata and big Awa, Nata's one daughter still living at home. Madinè would go to the bakery for fresh bread, Ami would fix "coffee," and the little girls would perch restlessly on their mother's lap while she fed them coffee-soaked bread with a spoon. Then Ami and Madinè would leave for school and Aminata would take the twins to their grandmother Fanta's next door so she could do her work in peace. At about ten, when she went home to look after her own house, she'd leave the twins with Fanta. Most mornings I had classes, but I returned for lunch and spent my afternoons working at home. Twin-watching became my favorite sport.

Twins really are different. Their little society is so complete and so fulfilling that they grow up socialized from the very beginning. Adame and Awa were never apart. They jabbered constantly to each other in a language no one but they could understand. They hid from each other in cardboard boxes and played house together with their headless dolls. Mostly, though, they just ran around the yard (they never walked), playing a kind of follow-the-leader. One moment, Adame would lead Awa along the low dam El Haji had built to Adame would lead Awa along the low dam El Haji had built to keep water

121

from entering his warehouse. The next, Awa would crawl under the laundry drying on a branch, and Adame would follow her. Now and then, one of the two would reach out and swat the other for no apparent reason, and both would laugh. Sometimes they called each other by name, but most often they simply shouted, "Twin!"

At the start, I was tempted to address them in the same way, for they were—and still are—so nearly identical that the only sure way I could tell them apart was by that little scar on Awa's forehead. Then one day Badara accidentally hit Adame on the forehead with a small stone aimed at Madinè, and even that clue was lost.

For a while, I thought differences in their behavior might be my answer. They napped at different times, Awa after her midday meal, Adame so late in the afternoon that she could hardly be waked when it was time to go home. Adame seemed bigger, stronger, and more aggressive, too. This last observation was confirmed by Aminata who explained that Adame got a head start during her first six months when Awa's growth was slowed by sicknesses.

But this notion, too, proved unhelpful when I saw one day that Awa was becoming more aggressive while Adame cringed pathetically in the background, waiting for approval. And sure enough, Awa was now huskier and perhaps a centimeter taller that Adame. This oscillation of size and assertiveness kept on for a year or more, each swing lasting for a month or so: the smaller twin seeming instinctively to sense her inferiority, while the stronger one strutted like the top hen in the flock. Of course, I couldn't just watch this happening because I was trapped in the subjective middle, as no self-respecting psychologist would ever be. So I kept mucking up my informal research by building up the confidence of the one while trying to moderate the dominance of the other.

It didn't take long for Adame and Awa to lose their fears of their American grandfather. Sometimes I wondered if they didn't lose their respect for him as well. Within months, lunch at Fanta's became an almost impossible ordeal. I usually returned from ENSup too late to share lunch with the family, so I was obliged to eat my rice alone. Well, not really alone. Adame and Awa, already fed and invigorated, would decide to eat again from my bowl. Then they would climb onto my lap, my back, my shoulders. Nobody seemed willing to stop them, and they were so affectionate, so clearly glad to see me that I couldn't bring myself to behave sternly enough to stop them either.

They were not entirely undisciplined, however. In the afternoon, Madinè would usually bring them to the house for a visit and, before entering, each little girl would take off her plastic sandals, called "flip-flops" in the U.S., and place them neatly beside the door. The last one inside always closed the screen. In the house, they would contentedly turn the pages of magazines or look for photos of Ami and Madinè in my album. Only occasionally did they mistake grandpa's living room for a gymnasium.

One of Ami's regular chores at the end of the day was to spruce up her little sisters before returning them to mother for the night. She'd plop them one at a time into a big plastic washtub, douse them with a pail of cold water (warmed in winter), and soap and scour them as if they were pots. Then she would polish them with oil and put each into one of the identical dresses she had washed and ironed so they would arrive presentably at home.

For the first few months after my return, Ami and Asa, the servant girl who helped look after Fanta during the school year, carried them the two kilometers home on their backs. Before long, though, the twins insisted on walking at least part of the way.

The Older Girls—Big Awa, Fatoumata, and Sali

"Big Awa," as we had to call her to avoid confusion with her new little sister of the same name, was indeed big—broad-shouldered, full-breasted, and as strong as a bionic ox—a typically Bambara young woman in spite of her admixture of Fulani blood. Nata guessed that big Awa was about seventeen (no one here keeps track of their own or their children's ages), but my own guess, based on the layer of baby fat that still clung to her circular face, is that she was closer to sixteen. Big Awa left school after finishing the eighth grade, not at all unusual for Malian girls, and spent her days helping her mother at home and braiding the hair of her sisters and friends. She gave me the initial impression of being a simple, dutiful daughter, stolid and reliable.

But Awa's placidity was deceiving. Nata told me with some concern that Awa's father had several times introduced men whom he thought would make suitable husbands for her, for she was just on the brink of the marriageable age, and each time she had refused point-blank.

"When I take a husband," she told her father boldly, "I'm not going to work in other people's houses like mother does. I'm waiting for a man who is rich enough so I can work only at home."

Actually, Awa might end up making more money outside the home than her mother does, for she was on her way to becoming an accomplished *coiffeuse*, a hairdresser. Malian women are somehow unable to grow long hair, so the women and adolescent girls buy skeins of fine black thread and have friends and relatives or, less often, budding professionals like Awa interweave it with their natural hair, usually in quite intricate patterns. Awa learned to braid her sisters' hair for all the big feast days, and her skill and sense of style led her to acquire a few paying clients as well. For Christmas, I gave her an oversize picture book with several hundred photographs of "Coiffeurs of Mali," which I found at the local tourist office.

Everyone in the family, boys as well as girls, was good-looking and well-formed, but the acknowledged standard of beauty was Fatoumata, who was just ahead of Awa in seniority. Once when Ami had especially delighted me with a display of her keen intelligence, I told her she was beautiful, for intelligence at work really is lovely to contemplate. She was embarrassed by the compliment. "Oh no," she demurred. "I'm not beautiful. It is Fatoumata who is beautiful."

Fatoumata, or "Tata" as she is called at home, was a tiny girl, hardly five feet tall in her sandals, with large eyes, curly black lashes, a turned-up nose, and small, perfectly formed lips, which she used to paint lightly with henna. She was diffident and rarely smiled, at least in my presence, but on those rare occasions when she did she looked like an ad for Pepsodent.

During the first months after my arrival, Fatoumatou was living at home with her mother, but used to come over once or twice a week to help with the laundry. I supposed she was about nineteen, and I was terrified of her shy seductiveness.

I wasn't the only one to notice this quality, and Nata often confided in me her eagerness to marry Fatoumata off before one of the local predators got her into trouble. Well, she can stop worrying now, because Fatoumata was married on my first Thanksgiving back to the eldest son of a rich Bamako merchant. Everyone hoped that she would now be able to help out her unfortunate older sister, Sali.

During my first two years in Bamako, I saw Sali only twice, when she came home from Saudi Arabia to display her newborn babies. She wore beautiful clothes and brought with her extravagant presents for the family—toys, clothing, a video player, even a refrigerator for her mother. Her husband Buacan had what everyone imagined was an indestructible job as chauffeur for the Malian Embassy in Jeddah, and I thought that Sali was not being merely generous, but was showing off.

One day, however (as the story goes), Buacan's widowed mother decided that she wanted her son beside her during her final years. It wasn't just that she needed money, for Buacan was treating her even more generously than the rest of the family; she wanted *him*. As a respectful Malian son, he felt he had no choice but to obey, and so returned to Bamako with his wife Sali and their two children.

In Bamako, where unemployed chauffeurs are still a dime a dozen, Buacan never found another job, and Sali was forced to sell off her new possessions to help keep the little family.

124

Their Parents—Aminata and Aliou

I must not leave the impression that Aminata, the mother of these nine children, was somehow less a mother because she left the little ones with grandma all day and the two schoolgirls with Fanta for years at a time. Fanta was—and is—a powerful force in shaping their characters, especially Ami's, but Aminata, or "Nata" as everyone calls her, was by no means invisible. Nata had never been to school and could neither read nor write, but she wanted her children to be educated, and once a month she diligently walked to their school, which is a mile and a half from her home, and talked with their teachers. She worried about Fatoumata's virginity, and then about Awa's celibacy and Sali's poverty, and she kept prodding me to help Salis husband find a job with the Peace Corps.

Aliou, Aminata's husband and the children's father, was a good-looking, quiet, and intelligent man, easy to imagine as the father of girls and of a gentle boy like Bua. A mason and often between jobs, he spent less time drinking tea and hobnobbing with his cronies than most Malian men, preferring to watch television at home or attend prayers at the mosque. The children feared him, but it was hard to imagine why, he was so mild-mannered. Even Nata never addressed him or spoke of him by name; in his family he was known only as "Papa."

Malians are infatuated with children and, like Aliou and Aminata, rarely count in advance the costs of feeding, clothing, and educating them. God, they assume, will provide. Well, He can't do it all, and the enormous families so deplorably common here are surely just as responsible for the nation's poverty as its inhospitable geography. At this stage in my relationship with the family, I was skittish about criticizing a practice so ingrained, but later, when I found myself wanting to help out with the medical and educational expenses of lovable child after lovable child but unable to do so, I became more forthright. Today the older girls talk sagely of a three- or four-child policy.

An Ecumenical Christmas

One of my first official functions as the children's putative grandfather was to escort Badara to the Christmas pageant sponsored by the combined kindergartens of Bamako. Badara's *jardin*, like most of those performing on the program, was secular, but the students and teachers were almost entirely Muslim; most of the small minority of Christian parents in Bamako send their children to one of the city's two Catholic *jardins*, and both of these were also represented. Two imams shared the podium with a nun and a red-hatted monsignor, and on the far wall of the sports arena where the event was held, a great red-and-white banner proclaimed in French, "The Mosque, the Church . . . Nests of Solidarity."

The entire program of songs and dramatizations was conducted in Bambara, except for a few dances and brief introductions in French, so I understood little, but the actions and gestures made it clear that the occasion was less a traditional celebration of Christmas than a semiofficial push for moral "*solidarité.*" Badara's group dramatized the marriage of a Catholic boy, Jean, and a Muslim girl, Fanta. While this significant event was taking place, the little grandson I had gone expressly to watch was nowhere to be seen; he had hidden himself behind his taller classmates and remained invisible and inaudible throughout.

Barely a tenth of Mali's population is Christian, but Christianity is highly visible in Bamako, and not just at Christmas time. One of the most conspicuous buildings downtown is the red-brick Catholic cathedral; next to this a Catholic mission, and there are three or four evangelical Protestant missions not far away. And in the bush, missionaries, including devoted agents of Jehovah's Witnesses who annually distribute millions of comic-book versions of the life of Christ, with text in Bambara, are still hard at work.

Ramadan and a Lesson on the Burdens of Beauty

The big religious holiday in Mali is not, of course, Christmas, but the Feast of Ramadan, which brings to a close the obligatory thirty-day fast called Karim. During this fast, no Muslim may let food or water pass down his throat between sunup and sundown. Exceptions are made for the ill, for pregnant women and nursing mothers, and for students taking exams, but most of these last try to tough it out. This year, fasting was especially difficult because the thirty days of Karim began in early May and coincided with the hottest season of the year. Temperatures averaged well over 100 degrees Fahrenheit during the day, and my eleven o'clock classes were peopled with zombies and so, I'm told, were many of the offices. Evidently a practice that caused no problems in a sheep-and-cattle-herding culture fourteen hundred years ago has not been adjusted to the demands of the modern world.

Madinè and Bua made valiant efforts to fast with their elders. Madinè's fast lasted until noon of the first day. Bua hung on for three days longer. Ami, who had been through all this before, just laughed and ate normally. Even she, however, refused to take her usual eleven-o'clock snack to school for fear of ridicule.

Like the American Christmas, Ramadan is the traditional gift-giving time of year. This year, I decided to do something special for Ami, for once again she was leading her class in the Qur'anic school. We went shopping together and, in a small boutique near the cathedral, found what amounted to a transformation—a modish skirt and matching jacket of blue denim, or rather, something lighter that looked like denim. I had become so used to seeing her in the same kind of ankle-length wraparounds that her mother and older sisters wear that it was quite a revelation to see her looking like a junior-high-school student in Amherst, Massachusetts. Ami, who radiates the genuine beauty of intelligence and character but has never considered herself in the same class as her sisters, was likewise enchanted by her new image, which was quite in the mainstream of teenage fashion in Bamako.

Unhappily, Madinè, who may be even brighter than her big sister, failed to pass the fourth grade and brought home a note citing her for carelessness and sloth. This was no surprise, really, as Madinè was terribly spoiled at home. She was almost never asked to help Ami with the laundry or even the sweeping up, but spent most of her free time gossiping with girlfriends or playing dolls with the twins. Often during our evening study hours she would fall unwakeably asleep long before her homework was done.

Madinè's failure had consequences for her. Not only did she not receive a celebratory present, but she was bundled off to spend the summer helping her oldest sister Sali who is pregnant again. Sali, Nata assured me, would see that Madinè now did all the washing, cooking, and cleaning up that her culture expects a girl often to do. Fearful that her doting father would continue to indulge his irresistible daughter, I sent him word through Aminata that, should Madinè fail again, it would be up to him to pay for her school. I hoped this would have some effect.

Madinè herself was overjoyed at the chance to spend the summer with Sali and her babies, no matter how hard the work, but no one else was happy about it. She is a gifted little girl, gifted not only with grace and beauty, but with an effervescent personality that brightens the hours of everyone around her. She had been gone only three days when Ami and I confessed to each other that our mornings and evenings had become impoverished without her. I wrote a short poem in her honor, my first new work in many months.

BEAUTY

For my granddaughter who has
just failed the fourth grade

O, beauty, beauty, beauty—what a cross,
what a curse to be born with!

Look at you! Not ten years old
and already you are scarred

127

by loveliness, afflicted
with the suppleness of wind

and the gazelle's grace! Laughter
falls out of you randomly as rain,

and nobody helps. Teachers
wink at your lessons, mother sighs,

father smiles at your lazy ways.
Soon beauty will tease you

out of virtue, catch you
a worthless husband

who will love you every morning
and beat you every night.

Listen, girl,
let beauty go as it will,

grow warts
while you can, pick up a limp

or a squint, play football,
write poems, kiss a frog

or a prince. Learn, child, learn:
beauty is always less than enough.

13

Explosion!

History didn't let me bask long in the warm sun of family make-believe. The waves of democratic aspiration that had been rocking eastern Europe began, in the late months of 1990, to lap at the river banks of Bamako itself, quietly at first, then with increasing force. In November, the previously discreet rumblings of popular discontent with General Mousa Traorè, Mali's corrupt dictator, erupted into violence.

For years, the government had ignored the unchecked growth of the downtown market center of Bamako. The once-orderly collection of licensed shops and stalls that furnished most of the populace with their basic needs for shoes, cloth, linens, hardware, cookware, and bicycle parts was first infiltrated, then invaded by hordes of petty, unlicensed sellers, mostly women, peddling their goods from makeshift tables crowding the streets and sidewalks around the central market. So dense was the crowding that even pedestrians had trouble passing from one street to another, and for vehicles passage was almost impossible.

Belatedly, General Traorè was persuaded to put an end to this intolerable situation, and he did so with the tools dictators know best—force and bluster. First, he ordered the sellers to move, and, when they refused to surrender their sources of livelihood, he ordered the police and the army to evict them. Brigades of armed men were covertly mobilized and, early one Monday morning, carted into the area with orders to remove or destroy all of the offenders' tables and merchandise.

Predictably, it seems now, the hundreds of small sellers refused to budge. Fists were thrown, then rocks, and within minutes scores of discontented young people and what Mali's government-controlled newspaper called "vagabonds" had joined the rock-throwing melee, indiscriminately attacking ministry buildings, telephone booths, and everything else that looked official. A number of government automobiles and trucks were overturned and burned until the demonstrators were finally calmed by tear-gas grenades and mass arrests. It was quickly clear that the table-sellers had the support of the citizenry, which saw them as heroes defending their daily bread, and the authorities were obliged to postpone the eviction.

Apparently, the General was completely surprised by the strength of feeling against him. As the new president of the Organization of African States, he had been out of the country a good deal, traveling around West Africa on "peace keeping" missions to Liberia and various other troubled countries distant from Mali and building up a high profile as an African statesman. Many thought afterwards that he had become over infatuated with his new image as a "leader of the free world" and was therefore unwilling to take the decisive actions that might have cooled the uprising at the start. Perhaps this was also why, after some twenty years of absolute censorship, he had just begun to allow publication of a few small independent newspapers.

The fat, however, was now in the fire, and the hitherto quiescent opposition lost little time in bringing matters to a head. A week after the confrontation at the market, a "March for Democracy" was called and at least ten thousand courageous citizens paraded through the streets of Bamako demanding, for the first time in public, the resignation of General Traorè and the installation of a multiparty system of government.

This was a startling denouement to General Traorè's proud reign as president of the Organization of African States, and seemed to catch everyone by surprise. Dire rumors were everywhere. Truckloads of riot police, armed with shields, tear-gas grenades, and Kalashnikov rifles, rolled into the city from the nearby military base at Kati; absenteeism was rampant in the shops and offices of center city, and many parents kept their children home from school. Peace Corps volunteers and other Americans were specifically enjoined from showing themselves near the line of march.

On this day at least, these precautions proved unnecessary, and the demonstration was indeed a peaceful one—the last peaceful demonstration the country was to see for some time.

130

Violence on Martin Luther King Day

Early each year, the American embassies in black African countries gear up for special celebrations of the birthday of Martin Luther King, the great black American hero of nonviolent protest. There are receptions at the homes of the American ambassadors, films, exhibits and special programs at the libraries of the U.S. Information Service, and, in Bamako, presentations by the English-speaking students at ENSup.

This year, two days after the outbreak of shooting war in the Persian Gulf, the two hundred odd students in ENSup's English department gathered in the school auditorium for a program presented by the English Club. Individual students gave speeches, well-researched but distressingly long, on King's life, on his spiritual debt to Jesus, Gandhi, and Thoreau, on the history of the civil rights struggle in America, and on other related topics.

King's message must have seemed to most of them—as it did to me—poignantly relevant during these days of confrontation, and the audience responded warmly when four students presented original poems urging world peace and brotherhood. Then, as a climax, an informal chorus of my second-year students sang out an enthusiastic version of the classic "We Shall Overcome." When they got to the verse "black and white together," several score rushed into the seats and dragged me forth to join them. Less than twelve hours earlier I had been listening to commentators gassing away on BBC and Voice of America about the threat of a worldwide "holy war" pitting fanatical Moslems against the "Satans" of America, and here I was, the lone white American presence in this black African, almost totally Muslim audience, caught up in a spontaneous demonstration of solidarity and love. I felt then, as I do not always feel, that love will conquer all.

But what a forlorn hope! As we filed out of the auditorium, word reached us from center city that, just as our King program was getting underway, a new pro-democracy march had been broken up by soldiers firing tear-gas grenades. Hundreds of other soldiers were raiding various schools in Bamako, including those of Medicine and Administration, to seize two dozen students accused of being leaders of the protest. On the next day, goons from "the Party" violently broke up a meeting of the determinedly nonviolent opposition; Amadou Sidibè, one of my colleagues in the English department, was badly beaten.

When news of this incident last arrived at ENSup about nine o'clock the following Monday morning, it spread through the classes like a train of lighted gunpowder. Cries of "Strike! Strike!" filled the air and, before I could take in what was happening, hundreds of students from all departments were rushing past me through the halls and down the stairs to the street below. There they muddled confusedly, shouting incomprehensible slogans while I watched from the comparative safety of a third-floor balcony. But no place was really safe. Shortly, a truckload of soldiers arrived below and began launching tear-gas grenades into the crowd. Then, as the students fled, a few grenades followed them into the courtyard of the school, so all of us got a good whiff of le gaz lacrymogène.

Still, it was not until I got home a little before noon that I realized how serious the situation had become. The protests were now citywide and by nightfall would be nationwide. Far too numerous for the army to handle, the angry demonstrators were now in clear control of the streets everywhere. From my house a kilometer or more from the center of town, I could hear strident voices shouting "A bas Moussa!" ("Down with Moussa!") One group of students from the lycée Bouillagui, marched right by the Peace Corps office two blocks away, now closed up and locked. The most violent confrontation was downtown at the war memorial near the Ministry of Education. This time, soldiers fired not tear-gas grenades, but real bullets, and four students were killed.

The following day, the government closed all the schools in the country, bringing a welcome reprieve that no one believed would last long since there were still demands outstanding for political and economic reforms and, especially, for an investigation into the shooting of students during the demonstrations. General Traorè was refusing to listen to any of them.

"Before I allow a multiparty system in Mali," he said in a broadcast address from the palace, "I will see you all in hell." To many students, this had the ring of prophecy.

The closing of the schools did little beyond concealing the gravity of the situation. Respect for the police and the military declined to a low ebb and was soon converted into open hostility. Bands of students, now released from their classes, gathered daily in the streets outside government offices, shouting new slogans and demands. Confrontations were frequent and many policemen, fearful for their safety, absented themselves from their jobs, leaving the streets to the students and to those whom General Traorè kept calling "vagabonds." On the Monday after Martin Luther King Day, the country's only permitted trade union joined in a general strike, and army bases nearby rushed tanks and foot soldiers into the city while high-school and junior-high-school students armed themselves with stones and homemade Molotov cocktails. A fever for revolution was spreading like cholera through the country.

From this time on, events moved with such swiftness, and communications were so haphazard, that it was hard to know what was happening until everything was over. Like all Peace Corps volunteers in Bamako, I had been advised to lock myself indoors and not to venture into the combat zone, which was just a few blocks away. I was given a walky-talky radio to reach the embassy in case of emergency, but what anyone there could do to protect me was unclear. Anyhow, this had become my neighborhood and I felt confident that, whatever grievances Malians might have with one another, I would be protected as a friend.

From behind my garden wall I could hear frequent bursts of machine-gun fire and the dull thump of exploding tear-gas canisters, and now and then a taxi or private car, pressed into service as a makeshift ambulance, would careen wildly by, honking loudly. It was evident that something terrible was going on almost under my nose, but what that terrible something was I could not know. Even for rumors I had to rely on brief, often contradictory bulletins from BBC and Radio France International and on occasional students who stopped by to see if I was all right.

The conflict was bloody but mercifully brief. Three evenings after the rioting started, frustrated by darkness and my inability to find out what was really going on, I had gone to bed early after scraping together supper of rice and curry sauce in Fanta's yard. It seemed I was barely asleep when I heard an excited rapping on my bedroom window blind. Ami and her older sister Hawa, now back at Fanta's, were shrieking to wake me with the news that General Moussa Traorè had been overthrown. Unthinking, I rushed out into the street to listen with a dozen or so neighbors to a great Babel of voices from downtown, like a noisy New Year's Eve on Times Square. A few red flares passed overhead like Roman candles, but I heard no more gunshots. Suddenly I realized that I was wearing only my pajamas and beat a fast retreat into the house. Mali radio was off the air and there was no way of knowing what was happening, so I waited for the morning news.

When morning came, everyone was too excited to have breakfast in the house, so we dragged chairs outside and had our coffee in the courtyard, with bread I had bought and frozen on Sunday. Radio France International confirmed the grapevine: A small group of army officers, sickened by the slaughter that the frantic General was encouraging, and convinced that his cause was hopeless, had quietly moved into the Presidential Palace and placed him under arrest.

With Traorè's downfall, all efforts to maintain order collapsed like pricked balloons. Looting became no longer the province of a few "vagabonds" but was now a family affair, a socially acceptable way for the citizens to get back some of what had been embezzled from them over the previous twenty years. For this I had a ringside seat.

133

Early in the conflict, the leaders of the pro-democracy opposition had distributed a "hit list" of the principal profiteers in the government. One of these targets was a large grain storage facility a few blocks away; another was a wholesale parts depot on the very next corner, owned by the General's wife. The day after Traorè's fall, an almost endless file of men, women, and children, all in holiday mood, kept passing by my gate bearing tools, ladders, cans of paint, automotive rear axles, and huge sacks of rice, flour, and millet; some came in cars, some with donkey carts, but most carried off their bounty on their heads: They resembled nothing so much as a procession of ants removing eggs from a flooded burrow.

No one seemed immune to the temptation to take whatever could be carried. Nine-year-old Badara proudly presented me with a roll of aluminum foil he had filched from somewhere. I explained to him why he shouldn't have taken it and why I couldn't accept it, and then half an hour later his father showed up at the house with a two-hundred-pound sack of rice loaded on the back of his mobylette. During the night, Hawa must have used her mother's keys to open my kitchen door to a group of husky young friends, for on waking I found inside three huge, bakery-size sacks of flour.

The following morning was one of relative quiet and I ventured out to visit a fellow volunteer living in a three-story building a few blocks away. She too was just emerging from her enforced cocoon and was happy to share the panoramic view of central Bamako from her rooftop. Together we watched pillars of black smoke rising from burning cars and government offices, exchanged anecdotes of our adventures, and sniffed the acrid fumes of tear gas and burning gasoline, but it was not until my four-block trip home a few hours later that I realized how widely the trouble had spread.

The local market, which normally accommodates sixty or seventy petty merchants, mostly housewives with small heaps of vegetables piled neatly on shaded bamboo tables, had been senselessly ravaged—tables and sunshades wrecked or burned, the perishable merchandise scattered on the ground and left to rot. The Lebanese grocery where I buy such staples as beer, butter, toilet paper, and tuna fish had been totally sacked, along with the neighboring government Office of Financial Management. Two cars with government license plates had been overturned, dragged into the middle of the street, and set afire to serve as roadblocks against the military. And, as I turned into my own small street, I could see half a dozen frightened black faces peering out from behind the relative safety of my green iron gate. Fanta, Ami, Madinè, and a few of their friends had taken refuge there when looters attacked a grocery warehouse two doors away.

All Sunday afternoon we gazed over the gate at troops of pillagers marching out of the warehouse with cases of soft drinks and whisky, and cartons of

134

canned and packaged groceries. Eventually, someone unloosed an air conditioner from its moorings, and then a ventilating fan and a couple of commercial freezers, and carted these away. At one point, an armored car sped by firing wildly, but, judging from the muzzle blasts, mostly into the air. Otherwise, the looting continued undisturbed. It was not entirely disorganized though, for while individuals were scurrying off with their little treasures, a small team of purposeful young men were methodically tearing down one of the building's cement walls—the wall abutting Fanta's tiny house. They seemed to know exactly what they were looking for and exactly where to look, for in less than an hour four of them emerged from the ruins dragging a huge office safe.

The storehouse emptied, the looters sprinkled the walls with gasoline and set them roaring ablaze. Fearful for Fanta and her meagre possessions, the children and I carted mattresses, clothes, toys, pots and pans, sacks of rice, and everything else portable into my house next door. Here, I cooked up a family-sized pot of beans and macaroni and we all bedded down safely for the night, I in my usual bedroom, everyone else on mattresses on the living room floor.

The next morning the fire in the warehouse was still burning, but not too briskly, and we could see that Fanta's room was undamaged. The street outside, though, was an almost impassable shambles—cartons, cans, wrappings of all kinds, an emptied file cabinet with its records and folders scattered everywhere, and, of course, the looted safe. Fanta was in her element. By six in the morning she was out front with her bundle of broom straws, and by seven the area in front of her doorway and mine was swept as clean as ever.

There must be hundreds of Fantas in Bamako, men as well as women, for within three weeks of the uprising, Bamako began to resume an appearance of normality. The wrecked stores were patched up and restocked, and shoppers crowded into the markets to buy shoes, jewelry, and pretty clothes for the upcoming feast of Ramadan. Here and there, the rows of shops and stalls were interrupted by vacant shells, like missing teeth, where the old structures had been gutted beyond repair, but their places were quickly taken by sidewalk merchants selling much the same thing. Most of the surviving buildings bore crude signs lettered "Vive AEEM" (the initials of the radical student organization), and perhaps this was why they were spared, like the Israeli children during the Passover. There were no soldiers in sight anywhere, no armored cars.

14

"The Best of Times . . . the Worst of Times"

hen my second-year composition students straggled into the classroom on the morning of April 9, two weeks after the fall of General Traorè, a few of them still decorated with bandages, almost everyone was on hand but hardly in the mood for study. Yet study they must, for they had lost almost a full trimester and, if they did-n't make it up, they would have to repeat the entire year. I made a little speech about their achievement, reminding them that their problems and their coun-try's problems weren't going to vanish tomorrow and that what they had real-ly won with all their struggle was an honest chance to cope with them. Then I went round the room greeting and congratulating each student individually. Happily, no one was missing, though one young man, a student I had never really noticed before, wore a bandage on his head; he told us his wound was from a rifle butt.

It was immediately clear that we would have to disregard our textbook assignments. These young men and women, with homemade weapons and their own bare hands, had just defeated the tanks and automatic rifles of one of the most venal and well-entrenched regimes in Africa, and they could think of nothing else. So be it. Instead of following my prepared lesson plan ("Write a short paragraph comparing life in the city with life in the village"), they would write free compositions on what they themselves had seen and done during the conflict and what they saw ahead for the country.

In class a week later, I was greeted with eighty-one papers ranging in length from one to four pages, all neatly handwritten on pages torn from the students' copybooks. This could not have been an easy task for any of them, for the usual assignment for their class in "paragraph writing" was a single paragraph no longer than half a page.

But energy and desire can work miracles in writing as in almost everything else, and I found these first-person accounts so compelling that I gave the writers an extra week to correct vailed on half a dozen American colleagues to help me select those that told the story best. Then I arranged for the students themselves to read these to an American audience at the Embassy's cultural center. Here are a few excerpts:

"The students were the first to rise," wrote Moussa Diop, an able but self-effacing student who always sat in the back of the classroom where he was least likely to be called on, "but instead of listening to our demands, Moussa tried to intimidate us. 'The calves don't know the lion,' he threatened, 'but their mother does.' Now we changed our strategy of struggle. Nothing had happened after 41 days of demonstrations, so we said, 'Let's pass to the phase "Ground War,"' as if it were really a kind of "Desert Storm" in Mali."

Most fathers in this ultrasexist society discourage their daughters from continuing in school beyond the first few grades, so those girls who make it all the way to a school of higher education like ENSup tend to have very sturdy personalities. Aisha Ba was a small, large-eyed, fairly light-skinned young woman from the north of the country. Her perpetually amused smile suggested that she found her teacher and everything he said faintly ridiculous, but she was nevertheless an outstanding student.

"In the beginning," Aisha Ba wrote, "the members of AEEM (the newly formed student organization) held meetings at schools to decide what our demands would be and how we would organize ourselves. Then, on the eve of hostilities, we cut the traffic by setting fires on the roads; you could see smoke rising from the burning tires, wood and dry grass. In the morning, we met one another in front of different schools, with weapons consisting of stones, gasoline, matches and sand, and proceeded to the places to be destroyed. My group set fire to the offices of the UNFM (the government controlled women's organization).

137

"This event was like a civil war, a war between the army and the civilians (for it was not a problem of students only). Though it was tragic, it enabled Malians to overthrow their president in order to live the better life they have always been seeking."

The Battle of the Bridge

Over the years, Bamako, which means literally "the place where crocodiles bathe," has developed unequally on the opposite banks of the Niger River. The left bank, where I and most of the populace live, includes the railroad station, the main commercial center, and most of the government buildings and foreign embassies. On the right bank is the rapidly growing suburb of Badalabougou, the great auditorium of the Palais de la Culture (a gift of the North Koreans during the socialist regime of Modibo Keita), and the highway leading to the airport and places north, south, and west. At the time of the uprising, the two sections were joined by a single bridge, and it was here that most of the blood was shed.

"We were well-organized indeed," wrote Youssouf Keita. "The students and pupils living on the right bank of the river occupied L'Avenue de l'Oua, the bridge, and the Palais de la Culture. Those living on the other side blocked the main arteries, including l'Avenue du Fleuve and the Boulevard de l'Independance, preventing any traffic downtown. Our leaders gave their orders, and the demonstrators began breaking all that belonged to the authorities—cars, buildings, offices.

"Soon the police came with tanks, guns and tear-gas, and began firing. A tall man with a very black complexion fell near me, completely crippled by the bullets, his clothes covered with blood. I saw a score of others falling on the bridge, hurt in the head, in the foot, in the chest. My heart beat faster, my hair stood stiff, there was sweat on my neck, and my knees shook in my trousers. I was petrified by fear. I had never seen such a civilian massacre in our country before."

Aliou Sogoba taught beginning English in elementary school before his success in a competitive exam brought him to ENSup for training as a 4 teacher. He was one of six so-called professionals in the second year. "I can hardly imagine that such a cruel struggle could have happened in a well-known Islamic country like Mali," he wrote. "Students and pupils on my side of the river barricaded all the main roads, preventing cars, busses, lorries, etc. from passing. Pedestrians who wanted to reach their offices were forced to shout 'Down with Moussa!' or to return home. Soon, armed soldiers came from everywhere and began shooting but, as we were greater in number, we succeeded in capturing some of them and taking their guns."

For most of the year, Mahamadou Samakè earned only average grades in composition, but his report on the "Battle of the Bridge" reads like a military analysis. "From eight in the morning on Friday, students and soldiers battled face to face. Initially, the soldiers dominated the fight because of their weapons; they used tear gas to disperse us and grenades to keep us from getting close to them. When we noticed that their tear gas and grenades were nearly finished, we rushed toward them. This was a mistake, for their first fragmentation grenades landed in the middle of our fighters and made a lot of victims. We now realized how difficult and dangerous was the combat.

"Our second strategy was to attack and destroy everything belonging to the government, like the Palais de la Culture and the many gas stations owned by Moussa's friends and family. We put barricades across the streets to prevent soldiers from riding at us and then attacked them with the only weapons we possessed, stones. Their answer was violent and our casualties were enormous—more than twenty wounded. We fled, reformed, and prepared to attack again, but a rain of bullets and grenades forced us to change our strategy, so we attacked from different sides in order to encircle them.

"This third attack was a success. Their ammunition finished, the soldiers climbed out of their tanks and fled under a storm of fire from the Molotov cocktails we had made. The EOSY gas station was already burning, and we took the Palais de Culture from the soldiers' control. The bridge was already free, and to assure our control, we made a big fire at the entrance, leaving a narrow space so the ambulances carrying our wounded fighters could pass."

Kadiatou Mama Traore, usually called "Kadi Mama," was a tall, muscular young woman whose previous claim to my attention was that she had scored the come-from-behind goal that enabled her soccer team to tie for the class championship. Kadi Mama is clearly a romantic deeply indebted to Alphonse de Lamartine and Victor Hugo, but what I liked especially about her composition was the way she combined the free expression of her feelings with real concreteness of detail. After hearing her read the paper at the American Cultural Center, I told her she should give up soccer and become a novelist.

"On Friday morning, I was wakened by the sounds of gunfire; it was the army forces shooting at students and pupils. I immediately dressed and joined the others at the IMACY building. Although we had decided to act with the greatest care, the soldiers began to shoot. Some of our group were killed, others were hurt; among the wounded, some lost their arms, others their two feet; a great number lost their minds for a while because of tear gas. Stones were our only fighting weapons.

"At eleven o'clock, I decided to move to another place. A young shoe-cleaner followed me, but when we were crossing the road the soldiers fired at us. The bullets reached the boy, and he fell. Three students helped me bring him to the hospital Gabriel Tourè; he died fourteen minutes later. The hospital was full of dead and wounded, and parents and relatives were crying, trying to find their children, brothers or sisters. I saw one boy twelve years old with no feet; in one room I could count twenty-nine dead.

"Later, I knew not how, I found myself within sight of the still-burning shopping center Sabel Vert, with the people trapped inside. Whatever they did, they had to die; as I watched, a dozen of them tried to escape from the building but the soldiers shot them down. A sense of heavy gloom filled my spirit, a coldness, a sickness in my heart, a complete sadness of soul like no earthly feeling. What was this? Was it a war between people of the same country? I could find nothing to lighten the weight I felt. Then I recognized an old classmate. He had received many bullets in his stomach and had only a little while to live. He took my hand and said,

"'Kadiatou, I shall die, I must die of this fool's sickness. In this way, this way and no other, I shall die. I fear for what will happen, but I do not fear for the results of what has happened. A time will come sooner or later when you will have your revenge in some last battle with this ghastly enemy. You will see a multi-party system in Mali; Moussa and his clan will leave forever.' After these words, he died.

"I couldn't stop myself from crying. I cried like a fool. Two old women came and took me to their house; they put some water on my head and I slept for a while; in the evening I returned to my house. I swore I would never be interested in politics if an overthrow of power has to end in this way."

A few weeks after the reopening of ENSup, members of the new provisional government paid us a visit. Among them was a former colleague who was teaching philosophy here when I first arrived in 1983. He had just been appointed Minister of Education, and greeted me with a shout, "Namory, it's been a long time!" Hopes for the new government were high. This was a great time to be in Mali!

Stumbling Toward Democracy

Even the great numbers of dead—more than two hundred by an early count—and the several thousand seriously wounded—did not dampen the popular joy over the demise of the corrupt regime of General Traorè. What did temper this delight, though, especially among students and other more thoughtful people, was the fear that one military regime might be followed by another. The victory was won by the people, and with the blood of the students, but the coup de grâce was administered by a group of military officers who had been in Traorè's confidence. Once order was restored, would Colonel Tourè and his fellow leaders do as they had promised and turn power over to the pro-democratic forces that had led the uprising?

Astonishingly, they did precisely that. Within days of his installation as President of the Committee for National Reconciliation, Tourè delighted almost everyone by naming as Prime Minister and head of the provisional government Soumana Sacko, an experienced economist and reportedly one of the most incorruptible men in the country. Sacko, nicknamed "Zorro" by the press here, had been fired as Moussa Traorè's Minister of Finance and driven into exile when he grounded at the airport a plane carrying 350 kilograms of government gold destined for his boss's personal bank account in Switzerland. Zorro quickly put together his own cabinet of twenty-four men and two women, all with graduate degrees and, to the relief of everyone, only four military men among them. This provisional government was to serve for nine months while a new, republican constitution was being debated and enacted, after which Mali would hold its first multiparty elections.

In keeping with the new spirit of *glasnost*, the constitutional convention was to be broadcast live on Mali's lone television channel, so I prevailed on Fatoumata's merchant husband Boubacar to help me shop for a TV set, and, with the schools closed, the older children and I watched every confusing moment. (As I should have known from my American experience, television was later to have a profound effect on our family evenings.)

At the convention, there was some support for the American system of three independent branches of government, but most of the delegates had been educated in France and opted for the more familiar parliamentary system in which a prime minister, appointed by the president, ran the government with the approval of a national assembly.

A curiosity to me and to many observers from the "developed" countries where literacy is an essential if sometimes controversial requirement for voters was how a fair election could be conducted in a country where not more than 15 percent of the population could read or write in any language at all. This was solved by asking each voter to select (in secret) from among a stack of preprinted ballots the one bearing the insignia of his preferred candidate or party, and then, again secretly, to place that ballot in the box.

Awkward as this procedure may seem, most of the several hundred international observers who converged on Mali to witness this first democratic election in all of Africa agreed that, in the main, the voting was fair. This did not make the results acceptable to the losing candidates, however.

Also broadcast in its entirety on Mali's lone television channel was the riveting trial of the leaders of the army and the government charged with responsibility for the slaughter. At the end of the year-long spectacle, the red-robed and white-wigged judges found Moussa Traorè and two of his chief aides guilty of murder and sentenced them to death, but most people expect they will simply be allowed to languish in prison.

The sophisticated concept of a "loyal opposition" is not well understood or appreciated in most countries unused to democratic elections. From the moment the victory of Alpha Oumar Konare was known, the losing candidates and their adherents among parties began strenuously to undermine the position of the winners, even if this meant making Mali ungovernable. Their tools were the students.

With the taste of victory still sweet on their tongues, the Association of Students and Pupils (AEEM) refused to give up the power they had won with such heavy sacrifice. They naively demanded that the new government increase "scholarships" by 40 percent and award these regardless of academic merit. The government pretended to negotiate, but instead ducked the issue to the World Bank, which of course, would have to advance the money to pay for them. The Bank in turn found these demands totally unacceptable in view of the near bankrupt state of the Malian economy. At an impasse, the students turned again to strikes and to demonstrations that grew more and more violent. Organized bands of teenagers barred serious students like those at ENSup and other career schools from their classrooms and, when these tried to study anyway, attacked them with stones. I was obliged to send my students home when one of them received a nasty cut from a piece of flying glass.

I cannot remember exactly how many times the schools of the country were closed and then reopened that spring and summer—after three days, four days, after a week. Classes were catch-as-catch-can, accurate grading became impossible, and the year, and the year following, were declared "blank." That is, students who passed their courses were given their earned grades; those who failed were deemed not to have taken them at all. Nothing worked. Many of the younger teenagers (at this point one could hardly call them "students") actually seemed to be enjoying this long reprieve from discipline. Finally, after the fall of two of his appointed Prime Ministers and an attack on the building of the General Assembly itself, President Konare reached outside the political sphere and called on a wily old banker, Boubacar Keita, to take charge of the government.

Keita, whose deceptively avuncular manner concealed a steely toughness, wasted no time. He jailed the mob's most vociferous ringleaders, instituted suit for damages to state and private property, and ordered all of the schools in the nation closed for a year. This last was a fatal blow to the die-hard insurrectionists, for it meant that students would be deprived of their monthly stipends until the schools reopened one full year later.

The wily old banker had judged the situation well. There were protests, some vehement, at the temporary loss of scholarships, but the people, including most students, were sick of the continuing disorder and wanted to get on with their lives. A year later, the refurbished schools were quietly reopened.

For those of us closely identified with the democratic aims of the struggle, it was sad to see how quickly the heroes of the revolution were hornswoggled into becoming its villains.

There were bright spots, though. A few of my fourth year students took advantage of the hiatus to do months of extra research on their dissertations and turned in outstanding papers on difficult topics. Sinalè Dembele wrote about the recurring conflict in American government between Federalists and anti-Federalists; Sékou Doumbia sought to answer the question, "Why is Edgar Allan Poe more highly regarded in France than in America?" Kadiatou Bocoum, the widely traveled daughter of an airline pilot, sought to enhance her chances of finding employment after graduation by proposing a plan to educate women on the care of the environment; and little Aisha Ba, the young Muslim woman who had played such an active role in organizing the student revolt, wrote an extraordinarily insightful paper on the philosophy of the New England transcendentalists. All four of these students have since become my friends, and all four are now working at promising jobs, a rarity in this depressed nation.

15

Grandfather for Real

As the twins were approaching their fifth birthdays, their parents suggested they move in with their grandmother next door to me so they could attend the budget-priced jardin des enfants, a few blocks away. It was a convenient arrangement. Most mornings I walked the little girls to the jardin and, when I could, I picked them up at noon on my way home from work.

One noontime, I found Adame near tears. One of the larger boys had chosen her as a target for his bullying, and she didn't want to go back to school the next day. At home, Awa confirmed her sister's story, a family council was convened, and all agreed that it was up to me to call on the boy's father and persuade him to put a stop to his son's bullying.

As the one white parent in the kindergarten, I had more than a few misgivings about calling on a black father whom I had never met to complain about his son, but Aminata and the children were insistent; as a woman, she obviously could not, and her husband Aliou was working out of town, in Koulikoro. And after all, it was I who had registered the two girls.

At dusk the children led me to their schoolmate's house, which was quite nearby, and together we paid our call. Word of the unexpected visit spread

144

like wildfire through the house and the surrounding neighborhood, and soon a small crowd had gathered in the yard to learn why I had come, for an evening visit by a *blanc* was evidently a rarity, something that might inspire a story on long evenings in the future.

With my heart in my mouth, I walked around the yard, shaking hands with everyone, even the small children, one of whom scurried whimpering behind the cover of his mother's skirt.

I had prepared a carefully respectful introduction in French, but my fears were groundless, my excessive tact probably unnecessary. The father turned out to be a quiet and friendly man who took my intervention as a matter of course. He called his son over and spoke with him briefly in Bambara, and the next day the bullying ceased.

This was the beginning of a series of small events that signalled a significant change in our relationships. We were no longer playing at being family. We were approaching the real thing.

Another evening after dark, a terrified volunteer visiting from Mauritania was pursued into my yard by a deranged, perhaps drug-crazed man who insisted that I let him follow her into the house. When I refused, he called me a greedy *tubab* and drew a wicked-looking knife from beneath his shirt and threatened me. It was a sticky moment, for not one of the small crowd that had gathered to watch the excitement seemed moved to help. Suddenly Ami, not quite fifteen at the time, rushed from Fanta's house next door and thrust herself between the crazed man and myself, effectively shielding me with her body. Galvanized at last, the crowd led the man away.

But there were other events, less spectacular, that told me I might now have a chance, in distant Africa, to rediscover the intimacies of family life I had thought lost to me forever.

For years, Fanta's eyesight had been deteriorating, and with it her once indomitable spirits. She had long since given up shopping and cooking for herself and no longer saw well enough even to sweep the leaves from her yard or the windblown trash from the street in front. Deprived of her sense of worth and forced to rely on her grandchildren for the simplest chores, she now spent her days sitting alone and silent beside her open gate, for her increasing moroseness had driven away most of her old friends.

Fanta's blindness was by no means hopeless, for even in Mali there are French and French-trained surgeons who routinely and efficiently perform cataract operations on their elderly patients. The procedure is quick, relatively safe, and surprisingly inexpensive. Her family urged it and I was more than willing to pay the modest cost, but Fanta was fearful of hospitals and opera-

145

tions, and only after she fell to the ground while groping for a chair she could no longer see did she give her consent.

The whole business was as simple as we'd been told. The cataracts were removed from one eye on a Tuesday and three weeks later from the other. For her convalescence, we moved Fanta out of her room in the warehouse and into the relative comfort of my living room couch with its fan overhead. Madinè moved in on the floor beside her as a kind of practical nurse, and the twins, who were now on a curtailed spring vacation from their first-grade classes, decided they, too, should help out and moved into my bedroom to share my double bed.

Early that first morning I was gently wakened by the furtive sounds of little bare feet tiptoeing past my pillow, carrying Fanta's well-filled potty to the bathroom. I could hear them flushing the contents down the toilet and then scouring the empty container with soap and coarse natural fiber, all the while whispering to each other to be quiet. Finally, as they returned the freshly scrubbed potty to its place beside Fanta's couch, they caught my watching eyes and grinned. This was my first real experience as the master of an African household, and I decided I liked it.

The Grand Tour

For some time I had been hoping for a visit from someone in my Stateside family. I was seeing most of them in the U.S. every couple of years, but what I especially wanted was for them to come see me in Africa, to meet and be surprised by my African friends and especially by my adoptive grandchildren, for I had none of my own blood.

I knew that the cost of travel to Africa was beyond the reach of my children, but I had saved up a little from my monthly Social Security checks, and I offered to pay half the cost of a trip to Mali for my son Wally and his wife Donna. They could share the experience with the others.

When they agreed to come visit us the following Christmas, their African counterparts were transported with joy. Already they knew the names of every one of my children and could recognize them from their photographs, for family relationships are the very stuff of life to Malians and many a long evening had been shortened by trips through my family album. "Is this Wally?" "Do Wally and Donna have children?" "Are your daughters married?" "How many children does your sister Nancy have?" Their interest was sincere, their curiosity boundless. Now they were to meet two of their proxy relatives in person.

Unhappily, it was not to be. My son Wally was involved in setting up a practice in holistic therapy and, a few months after accepting my invitation, was forced to beg off. What was I to do? I had budgeted the money for the trip. Mentally, it was spent. On a sudden impulse I decided that, if I couldn't bring a bit of America to Mali, I would take a bit of Mali to America.

Bua was the obvious choice. This would please Aliou, the children's father, who was concerned about the future of his eldest son, now thirteen, in a family of mostly girls. "He needs an adventure," Aliou had told me a few months earlier, not thinking then of an adventure quite so grand as a trip to the United States: A weekend in the bush would have suited him just fine. In fact, what he really had in mind, I'm sure, was for me to give Bua the kind of attention I had been lavishing on his sisters. Ever since his childish peccadillo of a few years back, Bua had been a model of comportment and was constantly looking for ways to make himself useful around the house. He ran errands, repaired defective light switches, unclogged drains; there was no task he would admit was beyond or beneath him. If anyone deserved the adventure, it was certainly Bua. I chose instead the identical twin sisters, Adame and Awa, who were then less than five years old and could qualify for half fare. And besides, they were girls.

At the time I married, I was a very mixed-up young man, an unsociable dropout from college, the Boy Scouts, and the theatre, and far too young for the responsibilities of fatherhood. I suppose that marriage was my way of escaping the bondage of a loving but domineering father.

For reasons that I understand but dimly even now, I was never really at ease with the sexuality of my own two daughters when they were little. I couldn't interest myself in playing house or taking them shopping or buying them pretty clothes. I encouraged them with their schoolwork and their music and dancing lessons, but I seldom hugged them or cuddled them. They do seem to love me nonetheless, but it was, as I see now, a pretty sterile relationship, which hurt them and impoverished me.

Fifty years later, age and Africa have worked their wonders, and my "grandchildren" have helped me to rediscover joys I did not know existed. Particularly the twin girls, who now shared a loving intimacy with me I had never encouraged with my own daughters.

For nearly two years, they had been accompanying their mother Aminata each morning when she came to do my wash and clean my house, then staying on to keep me company after Aminata returned home at noon, for I seldom taught after lunch. It was a wonderfully easy arrangement, for the little girls were so sufficient unto themselves that they needed nothing from me but the security of my presence. Sometimes they played house with my chairs, tables, and bedsheets, sometimes they tried futilely to braid my white hair, but mostly they improvised parties in the yard, making rice out of sand and sauces and salads out of leaves and blossoms from the trees out front. Then they would drag chairs out of the house and a big carton out of the kitchen to serve as a table and invite me to share the repast, first warning me that I must not eat any of it, for it would make me sick. At the end of each day, they would wash the dishes and put everything back in place without being asked. When friends or students came to see me, the girls brought them glasses of cold water; if I wanted to read or work, they let me alone. Every day at about five-thirty, their brother Bua would stop by on his way from the nearby Qur'anic school to walk them home. No impoverished elderly American, however deserving, has ever had it so good.

It was now nearing time for another paid home leave and I calculated that, traveling with me, the twin girls could fly for almost the same price I had been expecting to pay for Wally alone. I sounded out their mother, then spoke seriously to their father Aliou. "We'll be back in six weeks," I reassured him.

"That's not necessary. Why don't you just leave them with your son in America? He can adopt them."

The ease with which he tossed out this delightful and totally unexpected bombshell astounded me. Only a few weeks before, he had confessed to me that for years he had been uneasy over his children's cozy relationship with a white American who was never seen to pray. Only when he learned from them that I never offered them pork to eat, in fact warned them off if a canned sauce contained even a flavor of ham or bacon, did he begin to relax his concern.

And it seemed that he and Aminata were serious. In fact the whole family thought an adoption by my son would be a terrific idea. No matter that Wally and his wife Donna lived in a tiny house without a spare bedroom for the twin girls. "They can sleep on the floor," said big sister Awa, and everyone agreed. The twins themselves were enthusiastic.

"But they will be homesick for you and for Africa," I protested.

Aliou, who is a hard-working man and a capable mason but unemployed five days out of seven, scoffed. "No one wants to stay in this country. And how will they be homesick? They will be living with your son and his wife."

Few things would have pleased me better than such a merger of families, but I doubted Wally and Donna were prepared to take on the responsibility of parenting a pair of five-year-old African girls, however willing the girls might be to sleep on the floor. I tried to explain how middle-class Americans lived, but the only American they knew was myself and my lifestyle was only a little different from their own, though certainly more comfortable. Their enthusiasm, whetted by television and popular perceptions of America as the land of opportunity, could not be dampened. Already, the children were back into my photo albums, squealing loudly in their native language and pointing vigorously at this relative and that.

148

"If Wally has no place, we could stay with Nancy. Or Jaymie. Or Joan."
I temporized. "I will write everyone that we are coming for a visit, and
then we will see what happens. Anyway, there is still the problem of visas."

And indeed there was. The nattily dressed young consul, probably in
his first posting and sure that every African applying for a tourist visa was
planning, once in the U.S.A., to jump ship and disappear into one ghetto
or another, could not be convinced that the little girls and their proxy
grandfather had no such nefarious plans. Point-blank he refused even to
consider our appeal. My record of five years' honorable service in the
Peace Corps and my sincere commitment to return did not interest him,
nor was he swayed by the improbability of my abandoning my work to
thrust two little black girls onto the unwilling shoulders of the American
taxpayer. He was immovable.

Well, there's always the ambassador, I thought. I had met him several times
in connection with my work at ENSup, and he seemed a reasonable man.
Alas, his reasonableness stopped short of making even a phone call to the
consul, for fear that his interest might be construed as pressure. I was left with
the one alternative open to every American in a hassle with the bureaucracy:
my congressman. Or in this case, my senator.

Bill Bradley, the senator from New Jersey whose name, "William Bradley,"
Aisha had once inscribed in her notebook, knew me not at all, but of course I
knew him, as did almost every other American basketball fan. I wrote him a
respectful letter, not mentioning the obvious, that the consul might have
reacted differently if the girls had been white. Two months later, I was invited
to a meeting with the ambassador and the consul and told that the girls could
indeed be granted visas, but that I must present them physically to the consul
immediately after our return.

This was easy to agree to, even though I thought it was silly. The usual
problem with my biennial visits to the U.S.—where to stay for six weeks
without wearing out my welcome, since I no longer had a home of my
own—was solved when Wally agreed to contact family and friends and work
out a punishing itinerary: fourteen stopovers in seven North Atlantic states,
forty days in all, and no more than three days with anyone. The day after the
consul at last handed over the children's visas, Aliou rode over on his
mobylette, the little girls perched happily on the jump seat behind him.
"You'd better take them now," he said. "You'll want to get them used to
American ways."

Well, that wasn't very hard. They quickly learned how to introduce themselves and say "hello," how to eat with knives and forks, how to use a tablespoon to twirl spaghetti into a neat ball on their forks. We even had a special
session on how to use toilet paper. When the day of departure arrived, the

entire family—siblings, cousins, uncles, and aunts—piled into two rented cars and took off for the airport.

I knew that, whatever adoption plans might be made in the U.S., the twins were going to return to Mali first, but their parents didn't believe this, and so the good-byes at the airport had somewhat the air of a final farewell, but a jolly one. The girls happily clutched their plastic sacks of coloring books and crayons donated by the airline, and a few small presents their parents had bought for Wally and Donna. Aminata had commissioned a local tailor to fashion two beautifully embroidered *grand boubous* in harmonizing colors and she instructed me to see that they changed into these first thing in the morning. "I want Wally and Donna to see them for the first time wearing something typically African." The robes must have cost her three months of her tiny salary.

Our trip together was an inspired and sometimes awkward adventure, for it was the first time Adame and Awa had traveled more than a couple of kilometers from their birthplace. In New York, Awa, her bulging valise balanced Malian-style on her head, managed to tumble gracelessly down the escalator of the Long Island Rail Road station. Then somehow the two girls got themselves locked into the ladies' room of a Pennsylvania Railroad train and had to be pulled screaming out. And finally Adame, whose only previous experience in deep water had been bathing herself in a washtub, fell into the lake getting into a kayak at my friends Dick and Sandy Garner's summer cottage in the Catskills.

Unfazed, the little twins traveled through one adventure after another—riding an arial tramway in the White Mountains, sleeping in an upper berth en route from Atlantic City to Burlington, Vermont, splashing in a Maine Lake, and cowering under sprinklers in the pool of the Christian Science Church in Boston. They developed a fondness for cornflakes, pizza, and Ben and Jerry's ice cream. And, since most Americans who met these young Africans for the first time had been expecting little savages, the little girls astounded everyone with the graciousness and instinctive good manners they had brought with them from Mali.

After each meal, they tried valiantly to wash the dishes by hand, and when frustrated by the omnipresence of mechanical dishwashers, quickly learned to load these and washing machines as well. They swept and mopped the floors several times a day, and, on the several occasions when we ate out, they helped the waitress clear the table and carried their own plates into the kitchen. Everyone loved them and they loved everyone and wanted to stay, but nobody was in a position to adopt them.

After the allure and excitement of America, the realities of Bamako were a letdown. During their visit to Vermont, the girls had been invited to spend a few hours in a beautifully equipped first-grade classroom in the affluent suburb of Charlotte, near Burlington. There was an aquarium in the classroom, with real fish in beautiful colors swimming freely about. There were maps and colorful charts on the walls and, in the center of the room, small desks for no more than twenty children. There were special teachers for music, art, and English as a foreign language. Most exciting of all, even the first-grade classroom had *two* computers for the children to use.

Now they were plunged into the chaos of their neighborhood public school in the Quinzambougou quarter of Bamako. No maps, no charts, no fish. Just one exhausted teacher dividing her time in shifts among the more than 150 children in her first grade class. Shortly after the school year began, I paid the twins' class a visit and thought they might have fared better in the desert schoolroom in Nampala.

Many parents and teachers agreed with this gloomy assessment, and there arose side by side with the wreckage of the public system a new kind of school that was neither public nor private but an improvised merger of the two, called an "*école de basse*," or simply "primary school." Licensed by the Ministry of Education and obliged to follow the standard curriculum, these tiny new schools were organized for profit and staffed by young teachers eager to prove themselves in their first professional assignments. On the recommendation of friends on the faculty at ENSup, I took advantage of my grand-fatherly prerogatives to pluck the twins out of the moribund public school at Quinzambougou after one abortive year and reinsert them in the second grade of an *école de basse* which had just started up within a short walk from my home. So they moved back in.

And just in time. From their first day in the new school, it was obvious they had learned nothing during the previous year; they couldn't even read their own names. Fortunately, they were not alone. Fully half of their classmates had no business in the second grade, but had been passed along by teachers too busy or too bored to care. In a desperate effort to bring them up to speed, I engaged their teacher to come to the house after school for three hours a week, and on weekend mornings encouraged him to take over my own workspace with its built-in blackboard as a classroom for the twins and half a dozen of their more diligent classmates. (Because I was furnishing the room, the twins attended these classes free.)

Adame proved a serious student, practicing her numbers and syllables aloud for several hours every evening, and moved quickly up to grade level. Awa was—and is—more fun-loving and also perhaps less able. Both twins passed the year, but Awa just barely and I found myself wondering how long she could keep up the pace set by her sister.

There was no longer room in my life for loneliness, for I now had four voluble "grandchildren"—Ami, Madinè, Adame, and Awa—brightening my life

at breakfast and dinner and during the once-long evenings. And that wasn't
the end of it.

One Monday, a few months after the school term had started, Aminata
called me aside and confided with considerable embarrassment that the girls'
husky twenty-year-old sister Awa had delivered a bouncing baby boy the day
before. She claimed she herself had learned of the impending event only a few
days earlier. I saw no use in disbelieving this, perhaps it was so, and when
Awa's wrathful father expelled her from the house, she and her suckling infant,
called "Papa," took refuge with me and her younger sisters.

Papa was an incredibly beautiful child, like an interracial version of a
Gerber Baby Food ad, almost too beautiful to be a boy, with large, soft eyes
peering brightly from beneath his long, curly lashes, and so light-skinned that
I nicknamed him "our little tomacheq."

Not many years before, an out-of-wedlock birth would have brought
great disgrace on the girl's parents, and might have resulted in her permanent expulsion from the family. This is still often the case in the countryside, and peasant daughters are sometimes married as young as fifteen to
avoid temptation and shame. Not so in the cities. Finding an eligible husband among the swarm of landless, jobless young men may seem an almost
impossible job to many teenage girls and their parents, and today's rock-
and-roll permissiveness is no help to chastity either. The innocence that
Aisha had protested clearly belonged to another time and place, and most
urban parents know it. Within months Aliou let his rage soften and allowed
himself to visit his wayward daughter and to be seduced, like all of us, by
her irresistible child.

However, it was impossible for anyone to ignore the reality that, forgiven
or not, Awa had ruined her chances for a good marriage. As the virtual chief of
this growing family of girls, I made sure the lesson was not lost on her sisters.

There were now seven of us crammed African-style into my three-room
house. Ami, Madinè, "Big Awa," and her son Papa sleeping on thick blankets
and foam pads on the living room floor, and the twin girls sleeping alternately
in my double bed or on a pad on the bedroom floor. The intrusive presence of
the children's school gave a new definition to the phrase "rush hour." There is
just one bathroom in the house, opening off the one "official" bedroom—
mine. Ami, who sleeps on the floor of the living room with her older sister
Awa and Awa's four-year-old son, Papa, would get up first, around 5:30, since
she had custody of the alarm clock, and tiptoe into the kitchen to put water
on the stove for the little ones' baths. This is my cue to use the bathroom
while it is still possible; otherwise, I will have to wait in agony for forty-five
minutes or more before the toilet is free again.

I will then duck back under the sheets just in time for Ami to wake the twins so they can wash themselves from the pail of warm water she has brought out from the kitchen. When the little girls have been well scrubbed and oiled, Ami heats up more water and wakes Papa and his mother Awa so they can bathe as well. Meanwhile Madinè, who sleeps next door to keep her grandmother company, has bought the bread for breakfast and returned for her own bath while the twins take over the bedroom to dress themselves for school.

Once the girls are decent, I emerge from under the covers and, still in pajamas, stagger into the dining-room/workroom/classroom for strong coffee, which Aminata has arrived to prepare, along with tea and cocoa for the youngsters. The older girls spread the bread with butter and jam, and Madinè makes peanut-butter sandwiches for the twins and Papa to take to school, for Papa has been enrolled in kindergarten for the past month.

Finally, about 7:20, the five school-children shout their jolly goodbyes, the bathroom is free, and I take my own warm bucket bath. Until a month ago, I showered in cold water, but the unseasonably cold weather has made Nata's offer of a pail of warm water irresistible. A little before nine, big Awa takes off for work, Nata takes the laundry outside to wash, and I'm left alone with my computer. The rush hour is over.

Evenings before and after dinner mean more schoolwork, sandwiched between the children's favorite TV cartoons, dancing in synchrony with the television, and the news of Bamako in French. Adame is doing well in school, but her sister Awa is having problems. They may not be able to continue long in the same grade.

In spite of my bold dreams and strenuous bicycling, the years are beginning to press heavily on me. My internal health seems good, but everything is demanding more effort; even walking without a stoop requires me to give special instructions to my body. There are other signs of age—arthritic toes, a trick back, the kind of stiff knees that cost Mickey Mantle his job in center field and that are now making it difficult for me to rise gracefully from a chair.

To hide this last, I had developed a technique for springing nimbly upright by pressing my arms covertly against the chair seat and using them to push myself erect, much like the mechanisms devised to catapult old people to their feet. I thought I was getting away with this until one evening Madinè did an hilarious imitation of Namory rising and, when the usually respectful and sober-sided Ami roared as if she would split, I knew I'd been found out. Thanks to the magic of time and love, everything was now shared—even Grandpa's infirmities.

These infirmities were troublesome to my work as a teacher, so in the fall Peace Corps sent me to Washington to have the cataracts removed from my eyes. While I was there, doctors detected a hearing loss and I was fitted with tiny amplifiers for both ears. I was well on my way to becoming a bionic man.

16

"*Bless You Aminata*"

One reason that Peace Corps is such an effective agent for development is that volunteers are taught from day one that they are guests of their host country, and are there not to tell its people how to improve their lives, but to teach and inspire them do this for themselves. I followed this stricture from the very beginning, though it was not always easy.

When I took over the costs of little Ami's education in a Muslim school, I could have insisted that she go to a nonsectarian public school instead, and perhaps her devout, but impoverished parents would have listened to me. And perhaps they wouldn't.

Maybe I should have tried. But to me, the desire for an education was a value in itself. Time enough later to argue whether that education should be Muslim, Christian, or whatever. Besides, I did not appreciate at the time the many limitations of Ami's Franco-Arab schooling. What was important to me at the time was to foster the little girl's own natural love of learning.

There came a time much later, though, when, out of love, I chose to confront head-on one of Mali's most ingrained customs.

For three weeks of their summer vacation, the twins had been visiting their eldest sister Fatoumata and her merchant husband in the nearby suburb of Banconi. They loved staying there, for Fatoumata had three lovely children and a VCR on which they could watch thrillers, shoot-em-up westerns, and animated cartoons with no restrictions on the hours. Then, just as the girls were due to return, Aminata jolted me with the news that she and her husband Aliou had made an appointment for them to be excised the day following their arrival.

Excision has been wrongfully called "female circumcision" and consists of cutting away all or part of a girl's clitoris, in order to diminish her sexual pleasure and thus to assure her fidelity. It is widely practiced among certain West African peoples, including especially the Bambara, but there is increasing opposition to it among better-educated Malians who regard it— rightly—as a barbarism. Among my students at ENSup, it was a favorite topic for argumentative essays and debates. And now my beautiful eight-year-old "granddaughters" were to be subjected to this mutilating operation on the following day.

I was wild with concern and carefully controlled anger. For three years, Adame and Awa have been living with me, almost as my own children. I see that they are well fed and nicely dressed. I help them with their homework, pay for their schooling, including private tutors to help them survive in classes of nearly 100 children. I nursed them through chicken pox and tonsillitis. Why had I not been told earlier when there might have been time to do something about it?

For this last, Aminata had no satisfactory answer. Obviously, she and Aliou anticipated my opposition and had simply ducked the controversy in true Malian style by ignoring it. She tried to soothe my fears by assuring me that the old woman they had engaged to do the operation was very experienced and knew how to provide good sanitation and minimize the risks involved. "And she will cut off only a little bit, just the tip of the organ."

I was not at all reassured. The little girls, still ignorant of the ordeal ahead of them, were to arrive at my house that evening, on the eve of this irreversible change in their lives. What could I do to save them?

Not much, I feared. Aminata was convinced that the operation was absolutely necessary if the girls were to have any hope of finding husbands when they grew older. "Every girl in Bamako is excised," she insisted.

I knew this was not strictly so and that among educated families the practice was rapidly being abandoned, but Aminata, for all her native intelligence and her ambitions to see her children well-educated, was herself illiterate and traditional in her ideas. Her husband had not studied beyond the sixth grade, and no doubt most of their friends still followed the old ways. There was no convincing her.

To my every argument, she responded, "That may be true in America, but you don't understand Malians."

With less than twenty-four hours to go, I turned to my Malian friends at the Peace Corps, most of them with high-school or higher education. Everyone was sympathetic, but Sire Diallo, who had once played professional soccer in France and whose excellent English had earned him the job of liaison with the American volunteers, had a concrete suggestion.

"Just around the corner," he told me, "is the office of a woman lawyer who specializes in that very subject. In fact, she is President of the Association of Women Jurists, and excision is one of their main interests. Maybe she can talk to Aminata."

I wasted no time in hotfooting it over to Mme. Diallo's office. She was out, but her male secretary was in and made an early-afternoon appointment for Aminata and me to meet with her.

Mme. Diallo's office, just a few doors from me, was set in a beautiful small garden tucked out of sight at the end of a narrow alleyway. Hybrid roses, camellias, and a dozen other varieties of flowering and leafy plants surrounded a small patio and, at the time of our visit, colorful songbirds—yellow, indigo, orange, and red—were noisily feeding in the branches overhead. A few were evidently weaving their nests.

These signs of life and beauty were heartening, and I was especially grateful for them when Mme. Diallo failed to arrive at the hour of our appointment, or for nearly two hours after-ward. Aminata's day's work for me was finished and she was due home to do her own laundry and fix dinner for her husband and their three boys. I was afraid, though I needn't have been, that the wait would prove too long for her and she would have to leave with our errand unfulfilled. However, she must have known how important the interview was to me and, after an hour or so, stretched out on one of the patio's two padded benches and fell asleep.

A little after three, the distinguished jurist, for so she was, invited us into her office. She proved to be a large, handsome woman in her middle forties, with an open, sympathetic manner and a powerful presence. Her husband had been Minister of Health in the old regime of Moussa Traorè and she was obviously accustomed to authority. I presented the situation and, after the first few minutes, she spoke with Aminata in Bambara.

Whatever she said, and however she said it, her plea must have been effective. After about a half-hour's conversation, to which I contributed absolutely nothing, Mme. Diallo turned to me and said, "Aminata will speak to her husband this evening, and they will abandon the project."

Of course this is what I had hoped for, but after all the agony and the waiting, the jurist's brief announcement came almost too suddenly to be believed. I turned to Aminata.

"Is that true? And he will agree?" She nodded. "It is finished then?" She nodded more vigorously and smiled.

"It is finished."

Emotionally, so was I. I threw my arms around her and cried out, "Bless you, Aminata, I love you! You are a wonderful mother and a wise person." I murmured a brief but effusive thank-you to our benefactor and left before she could see the tears welling in my eyes.

Aminata, too, was moved by the occasion, for, as Madinè told me later that evening, she did not return immediately home but stopped next door at Fanta's to tell the twins' older sisters Ami and Madinè of her decision. Both girls, themselves veterans of the operation, told their mother that she had done the right thing.

Not an easy thing, though, and during the coming months and years, Nata will need all the reassurance she can get. Her husband, she told me when she came back to work the next morning, agreed to forgo the procedure but she herself was still worried about her daughters' ability to find husbands when they are older.

When the twins returned from their holiday in Banconi, blissfully unaware of the ordeal they had so narrowly escaped, they must have wondered why I celebrated their return with a special dinner of fried chicken, ice cream, and cake, and two candles on the table. I love these little girls and, if I were the praying sort, I would be praying now for my own good health and long life.

Afterword

This has been a difficult book to finish, for each day has brought changes, revelations, new ways of seeing the same old things. In any case, even the constellations among which I cast my line are changing: In the summer of 1995, Peace Corps officially ended its support for higher education in Mali, and that included ENSup's last surviving American teacher—me.

I might not have been able to stay on in any case. The heavy traffic in downtown Bamako was making my bicycle trips to ENSup more and more hazardous. I had already taken several bad spills and, just as I was about to leave on my forced retirement, I took another and was obliged to say good-bye to my frightened grandchildren from a wheelchair.

Fractured vertebrae was the diagnosis, and for six months I camped out in my sister Nancy's comfortable apartment in downtown Boston while I underwent neurologic treatment—mostly investigative stuff like MRIs, X-rays, and a spinal tap—and waited impatiently for the bones to knit, moving progressively from total bed rest to wheelchair to accompanied walks with a cane.

A lousy life for an old man with a passion for independence; without the understanding of my family and good friends like Stephen Dunn, it would have been intolerable. But they were there when I needed them and left me alone when I didn't, and after six months I was able to board a one-way flight back to Bamako—walking with a cane and with no job and no capital, but with $825 a month from Social Security and lots of that wonderful adrenaline that comes from desperation. My American children were financially independent of me and, at age seventy-eight, I had no wish to beat my head against the U.S. job market.

Of course it was another triumphant homecoming—six bright-eyed children peering past the customs barrier and waving frantically for my attention, and then all seven of us (eight including the driver) jam-packed into a tiny Renault taxi, with more friends, neighbors, and former students waiting in a spotless house. Sure of my eventual return, no matter what happened, I had kept up the modest rent and assigned the children as caretakers. All six of them have installed themselves there, claiming *droit de famille*, and now show no intentions of leaving.

Ami, Madinè, "Big Awa," and Awa's little boy Papa, sleep on a thick blanket and on foam pads on the living room floor, and the twin girls sleep alternately in my double bed or on a pad on the bedroom floor. The third room is kept sacrosanct as a combination of study for me and classroom for the children.

All day long, I live the lovingly protected life of a Malian grandfather. Beautiful small virgins (and some not so small) run my errands, bring me bread and cool water, sometimes beer; little boys insist on carrying my briefcase and my groceries. By rights, I should be on the threshold of poverty and despair; instead, I find myself halfway to Paradise without having stopped by Mecca or said my five daily prayers. How can I write or do anything useful in this state of undeserving-ness?

Ami is fearful that my euphoria will lead me into foolishness and has decided to take personal charge of the household money. She is almost exasperatingly frugal. Whenever I come back from the bank with cash, she counts the bills, gives me about $6 for pocket money, mostly for transportation and small repairs, and squirrels the rest away for food, soaps, and other household needs, and for notebooks and tutors. I've shown her how to keep simple records, but these are hardly necessary, she is so conservative and so meticulous. And it's good that she is, for ever since the devaluation of the Central African Franc, Mali has become an expensive country in which to retire, especially in view of the depressed value of the American dollar.

Thanks to Ami, our meals are cheap and pretty much the same every day. Breakfast: milk and coffee with bread, butter, mayonnaise, or jam. Lunch, supplied by Fanta: rice cooked with a sauce made from dried fish, peanut butter or simply oil and tomatoes, flavored with a concentrate, something like bouillon cubes. Dinner, prepared by the older girls, is our one daily extravagance: big helpings of french fries with lettuce and tomatoes vinaigrette; we used to accompany these with bread spread with tuna fish, onions, and mayonnaise (no celery here), but the worldwide fish shortage has tripled the price of canned tuna (even shrimp is cheaper), so mostly we make our sandwiches of fried plantains.

This may sound pretty awful, but we do have treats a couple of times a week—fish, barbecued beef, maybe a small chicken. Powdered milk (the only kind safe to drink here) is expensive, so we drink it only at breakfast, but every couple of days Nata makes us a pitcher of ginger lemonade. On Sundays, we buy seven eggs, and Ami makes a delicious "Western" omelet with onion, green pepper, and corned beef. One Sunday a departing staff member gave us a bottle of Log Cabin syrup and I taught Ami to make pancakes, for I am not allowed to do any cooking.

In fact, even my gentle suggestions are taken with ill grace. Ami and Madinè, who prepare our dinners, are used to cooking outdoors in heavy cast-iron marmites over a wood fire, and they insist on cooking the same way in lightweight aluminum pans on my gas stove. The burners are always turned up to high, no matter whether they are heating bathwater or simmering a slow-cooking sauce, so my pot handles have all burnt away and I am obliged to fry even my eggs (which I sometimes do on the sly) in an iron soup pot.

Medicine is not the heavy drain I feared it might be, cut off as I am from the Peace Corps' medical service and from Medicaid as well. Knowing of my predicament and my commitment to the children, Professor Ali Guindo, chief of Medicine at the Hospital Gabriel Tourè, volunteered his own personal services, and my only medical expenses thus far have been for drugs, x-rays, and consultant services, and these cost far less than in the U.S. Shortly after my arrival, five of the children came down with chicken pox at the same time, two of them with severe cases, and we didn't miss a meal.

The children's education is my big concern. Ami has just graduated from the twelfth grade of her Islamic school, but is finding out that her hard-won baccalaureate in Qur'anic studies can help her neither to a job nor to a higher education, but is useful only for reciting her prayers—a poignant victory after all her diligent work. She now wants to enter the educational mainstream, even though this will mean dropping all the way back to the seventh grade. So she has taken the exam that all public school students must pass at the end of the sixth grade in order qualify for the second cycle of primary school, what we would call junior high. But after twelve years as a stellar student at the Qur'anic school, she is finding the transition, at age nineteen, to the seventh grade of a French-speaking school a frustrating struggle and is showing signs of discouragement.

Her younger sister Madinè is in better shape. She, too, began her education in the Franco-Arab *mederasa* where her father enrolled them because, like many Malian parents, he believed that a study of the Qur'an was the only appropriate formal education for a woman. But Madinè, a resilient little beauty for whom I had predicted dire consequences when she failed the fourth grade in her Islamic school, has confounded expectations and is maturing into a very serious and determined young lady. While I was off convalescing in Boston, she persuaded her father to let her join the twins in their semi-public school where the language of instruction is French, even though this meant dropping all the way back from the eighth to the fourth grade, just a year ahead of her twin sisters Adame and Awa. Already she is the star of her classes in grammar, reading, and composition, though she had never studied French before.

Madinè has confided to me that she wants to become a schoolteacher, and, if determination is enough, she will surely achieve her goal. Each evening, while Ami is struggling to keep up with her lessons in French, mathematics, history, and geography, and after she has finished her own homework, Madinè reviews the lessons of her younger sisters and drills them relentlessly in spelling and arithmetic. She agrees, though, that she will have to curb her impatience and her temper.

Leaving the Islamic school was for Madinè a practical and educational decision, not a religious one. Three times a day, morning, noon, and evening, she leads her little sisters out into the yard, they cover their heads with makeshift shawls and, with little Papa joining in, they chant the Qur'anic prayers Madinè learned at the *mederasa*.

I encourage them in this. We are all children of the same God, though we may approach this God in different ways, and when my support is gone, the children will need all the strength their faith can give them.

The twins are not doing well in their classes and, looking back, I know I should have ignored their mother's tearful pleas and insisted they start first grade all over again in their new school. Instead, I let myself be convinced that a tutor coming to the house four hours a week could help them make up almost the entire first year's work in reading, writing, and arithmetic while continuing in their second-grade classes.

Well, it almost worked and might have if I had been able to stick around. With nightly drills, Madinè and I and "Monsieur" had just managed to shoehorn them through the second grade and into the third when I was forced to leave for the U.S. In Mali six months later, I am back at the same old stand, financing cram sessions so they can pass from the third grade into the fourth.

But I must stop talking about "the twins" as if they were one personality, for they are only as alike as two peas in adjacent pods. Awa is a live wire, much as Madinè was at the same age—playful, bored with school and housework, a little selfish, a fantastic dancer, always on the cusp of failure. Whenever I worry about her difficulties at school, I console myself by remem-

162

bering that her sister Madinè was doing just as badly at the same age and has now become the scholar of the family.

Adame is quite opposite—serious, reflective, and wonderfully affectionate, always anticipating my slightest wants. On a cold night, she will quietly creep over to my bed and adjust the sheet to make sure I am covered. And this Sunday morning, when the power went off just as she and her sisters were leaving to pick out their gifts for the feast of Ramadan, she placed the family flashlight on the chair beside me "in case you have to go to the bathroom in the dark." Adame is not a brilliant student, but I never fear she will fail.

In any case, success in school, however important, is no more the main criterion for success in life here than it is anywhere else. Character always counts most. Character and luck.

Many good things have happened in the country since the overthrow of the Traorè dictatorship and the installation of democratic government five years ago: Some of the tax money that used to be funnelled into secret bank accounts abroad is now being invested in schools, in health, in streets and highways; private investment is being encouraged; the small-scale civil war in the north that has been draining the country's resources for decades may at last be yielding to negotiation. Hopefully, the children will grow up in a healthier, more stable Mali than the one they were born into. Or their own intelligence and breeding and the wider experience I have furnished will guide them into the successful marriages that are the goal of all young Malian women.

But nothing comes easily here, and a century and a half of colonialism, handouts, and misgovernment have left their scars on the people as well as on the economy. Only this morning, as I was writing this, Ami came home in tears to tell me that striking students from the lycées downtown had invaded her junior-high-school classroom with stones and chased the young pupils out; their leaders are demanding that "scholarships" be paid monthly during vacation times as well as during the school year.

Whatever happens, I will have to comfort myself with the belief that I have been doing the best I can, or almost the best, to give this African family that has taught me so much about love a fighting chance to escape the life of ignorance and poverty that would otherwise have been their lot.

Africans are a remarkable people—intelligent, charitable, courageous. Deprived of those bounties of geography and climate that have propelled us more northern peoples to a faster development—exploited and degraded by others richer than they—corrupted sometimes by their own haste to catch up—they have nevertheless held on to their dignity and their humanity and their courage.

The people of Mali are survivors. For centuries, they have survived in a landscape ravaged by drought, famine, and plague. Year after year, like the

Keitas, they grub a meagre subsistence from their impoverished soil; they stand on their feet in the face of one defeat after another.

This is more than stoicism. It is a recognition that, even when overwhelming circumstances seem to have robbed them of all power over their lives, when there seem no hopeful new paths to follow or life-changing discoveries to make, a few small choices yet remain. Pitifully small, perhaps, but enough to keep alive the necessary illusion of freedom. And, like Aminata, they are capable of change.

Even the lucky ones among us, those who, like myself, have experienced nothing worse from life than its inevitable small sadnesses—losses, failures, separations, and disappointments—need to be reminded that courage and curiosity are both essential. Suffering and death are indeed the lot of humankind, but so, too, is wonder if we leave room for it.

About the Author

A former publicist and editor of The Menninger Quarterly, **DONALD LAWDER** has published poetry in The New Yorker, The Nation, The American Scholar, and elsewhere. He is the author of THE WILD BIRD AND OTHER POEMS, published by Sweetwater Press in 1993. He lives with six Malian "grandchildren" in a three-room house in Bamako.

Printed in the United States
39694LVS00003B/88